Staging
Dance

To Norman Morrice and Maria O'Connor

Staging Dance

Susan Cooper

Foreword by David Wall CBE

A&C Black • London
Theatre Arts Books/Routledge • New York

First published 1998
A & C Black (Publishers) Limited
35 Bedford Row, London WC1R 4JH
ISBN 0 7136 4489 9

A CIP catalogue record for this book
is available from the British Library.

Published in the USA by
Theatre Arts Books/Routledge
29 West 35 Street, New York, NY 10001

ISBN 0 87830 081 3

CIP catalog record available at the
Library of Congress.

Typeset in 10 on 11½pt Palatino

Printed in Great Britain
by Butler & Tanner Ltd, Frome, Somerset

Cover photos
Front Main photo by Pete Jones is of Cyn Dee Too in *Pleasant and Correct* by Kazia Rudewicz for Royal Academy of Dancing College Workshop '95.
Smaller photo (above) by Bhajan Hunjan is of 'fire' section from *Samsara* project 1995, showing the floor painting described on page 126.
Smaller photo (below) by Christopher Baines is of the Jiving Lindy Hoppers.

Back Photo by Focus on Dance shows Greasepaint School of Make-up making up a young dancer for *Horoscope* by Gail Taphouse.

FOREWORD

There is of course no substitute for experience, but to be able to share in that of others is invaluable.

As a young dancer, performing the roles of Siegfried in *Swan Lake*, Colas in *La Fille Mal Gardée*, Albrecht in *Giselle*, Romeo in *Romeo and Juliet*, for the first time, I had the help of not only the choreographers, choreologists and ballet masters but more importantly was able to share in the experiences of Rudolf Nureyev, David Blair and Christopher Gable. Their generosity in imparting their knowledge, expertise and enthusiasm helped me to sculpt my interpretations and gave me the security to become an artist, not just a fine dancer.

It is with this same generosity that Susan Cooper has written *STAGING DANCE*. She has such a wealth of experience and love for dance. She has covered in its pages the full spectrum of expertise needed to stage a performance, a unique book which I know will help and enlighten all who read it.

David Wall CBE

Contents

ACKNOWLEDGMENTS

Thanks are due to everyone with whom I have worked in the theatre – dancers, choreographers, directors, composers, musicians, designers, technical and administrative staff – and as a teacher. Particularly David Dean, who has inspired many creative activities, and Susan Danby, Principal of the College of the Royal Academy of Dancing for recognising the value of production experience in dance training. Also Christopher Davey, David Plater and Joy Duffett.

Special thanks to Darryl Jaffray, Head of Education, The Royal Ballet; Rachel Lightfoot, Rebecca Hanson, Bhajan Hunjan, Jo Maund, Tim Sutton, Jonathan Petter; Bill Cratty and Lars Jensen of Transitions Dance Company; Terry Monaghan and Eileen Feeney, The Jiving Lindy Hoppers; Fergus Early, Green Candle Dance Company; Lloyd Newson and Leonie Gombrich, DV8 Physical Theatre; Joyce Butler; Judith Maden, Arts Educational London School; Shân Maclennan, Royal Festival Hall; Bill Deverson, Blitz '96; Teerth Chungh, Cochrane Theatre; Val Bourne, Dance Umbrella; Annie Lincoln, English National Ballet; Glen Morgan; Peter Farley, Malcolm Stewart and Peter Docherty of Central Saint Martin's College of Art and Design; Mary Clarke; Mollie Davies; Ann Whitley; Stuart Beckett; Val Hitchen.

Royal Academy of Dancing, Chief Executive David Watchman, Carolyn Parker, Mandy Payne and students.

Cristina Aguiar, Paul Armstrong, Mike Concah, Dee Conway, Susan Crow, Gadi Dagon, Chris Davies, Focus on Dance, Hugo Glendinning, Tim Griffiths, Tony King, Martin Meyer, Chris Nash, Brian Slater, Anastasia Shorter and Angela Taylor for photographs.

Tesni Hollands and Anne Watts for all their advice and encouragement.

Introduction

> 'I never in my life set my feet on a stage without thinking of its magic and my destiny'
>
> Ruth St Denis in *The Art of Making Dances* by Doris Humphrey

My aim is to help you create the magic of dance onstage. Some stages you will encounter may appear, at first glance, to possess precious little magic: a freezing hall with a slippery floor is a typical example. The magic will certainly have to be created by *you*, both as a dancer and in how you adapt and make the most of the unpromising space.

An expressive body performing beautiful and exciting movements can be spellbinding in its own right without the addition of glamorous costumes or dramatic sound effects. However, most audiences expect to enjoy a dance performance complete with even the most minimal staging features: live or prerecorded music or sound, simple but effective lighting, and costumes which enhance the intention of the choreographer. They will expect the show to run smoothly: the dancers to be well rehearsed, the sound quality to be adequate, and the venue to have good sightlines. These expectations will prevail, whether they are watching a major ballet or a modern dance company in a well-appointed theatre with all the resources of regular funding, full-time staff and dancers, or at the other end of the scale, a small youth dance group with no funding or full-time back-up, and existing largely on the dedication and goodwill of its participants.

Compared with the other arts, dance is often treated like the poor relation in terms of recognition and funding, yet as an art form it uses the most basic form of human expression, the body. In its different forms, dance is practised and enjoyed everywhere, whether as a social, religious or theatrical activity, and every culture has its unique dance traditions. Only a few, however, earn a living from it, and for those who do, it is a short career.

One definition of the terms 'professional' and 'amateur' suggests the former has enough training and experience to demand and receive a salary, whereas the latter neither requests nor receives a salary for his or her work. In drama and music there may exist a clear dividing line between these two positions, but in dance there are many areas of work which fall somewhere between the two. A professional or amateur theatre group might produce *She Stoops to Conquer* or *The Mikado*, whereas only a professional ballet company will put on *Swan Lake*. In the specialised world of ballet, there is no equivalent to the tradition of amateur dramatics, so there are no dentists or florists by day who become Odette-Odile by night!

However many activities are being staged in a variety of settings in modern, tap, national and social dance, as well as ballet. Many young people today are engaged

1

in dance, whether as a hobby, at school studying at GCSE, A and AS Level, or undertaking professional training at a vocational school or on a dance degree. Whilst there is fine writing in books and specialist dance magazines on the individual aspects like choreography, design and music, relatively little has been written on all the staging elements together, in a practical format.

Like all theatre activities, a dance performance is the result not of one person's endeavour, but that of many, so this book is aimed not only at those on the dance side of a production, but also musicians and designers working alongside them, and those involved on the technical and administrative side.

Part One covers the different areas involved in the staging process. The practical suggestions are written at a basic level, and I have suggested sources of further information for more experienced practitioners. These include videos of dance works which illustrate certain aspects discussed in the text and which can give ideas and inspiration for more ambitious projects. Further reading is given at the end, and the names and addresses of supporting organisations.

Part Two gives examples of a number of dance companies and projects. It is hoped that they will show how the elements outlined in the first section work in practice. Every project and company works as a *whole*, with an artistic aim, group identity, and set of practical limitations. No single aspect of staging works in isolation from all the others. The book is concerned with practicalities, as determined by the artistic ideals which underlie them.

It is suggested that you read the whole book through, once, to get an idea of the overall process and the variety of situations in which dancemakers find themselves. Having had a taste of the opportunities and limitations you will encounter, go back and reread Part One, assessing how the information contained there can be adapted to your own situation.

I have assumed that you are without significant financial support for your work. In periods of recession, when the arts are often considered a luxury, the difficulty of finding resources can seem an overwhelming obstacle for many dancers. Excellent ideas and plans are abandoned in the light of problems associated with funding and organisation, and great determination and belief are needed to keep going. Courage, energy and inspiration can be as hard to find as cash! You need to find ways in which the production process can be enhanced, and limited resources used wisely and effectively. In the words of the popular song, you must, 'Accentuate the positive, eliminate the negative!'

The most positive aspect of the work of many dancemakers is the passion and joy it engenders, so the first and most vital element to accentuate and nurture is precisely this love. Throughout the creative process, there are pitfalls to discourage even the most dedicated and seasoned creator, so an encouraging and enthusiastic atmosphere is your most precious resource.

I hope the book will be a source of support at moments when the whole venture seems overwhelming. You will ask why you ever thought it was a good idea to attempt a dance performance! Many areas need specific expertise, and you may not possess these skills. Let's assume you are a dancer, choreographer or teacher who is donning another hat, as director or producer, and is responsible for the final result. In other words, the buck stops with you. In the event of a successful enterprise, you will doubtless be delighted to accept the credit, and maybe even a little financial reward. Along the way, you may rue the day you decided to be in charge – after all,

*Students of the Royal
Ballet School rehearse
Matthew Hart's* Sleepers
(PHOTO: *Focus on Dance*)

you're an ARTIST, and should not be expected to be every other expert rolled into one!

However, reflecting on dance history, it is evident that key figures frequently have been multi-skilled. Look at the achievements of Marie Rambert, Ninette de Valois and Martha Graham. They did not succeed by relying on one talent alone – all were dancers, directors and teachers, de Valois and Graham were major choreographers, and all had the ability to inspire collaborators, publicise their work, find funds, survive the lean times and live to a ripe old age. Their books, *Come Dance With Me* and *Invitation to the Dance* by de Valois, *Quicksilver* by Rambert and *Blood Memory* by Graham make stimulating reading, and the fact that events they describe took place some years ago, when conditions were possibly even more difficult than today, only adds to their value. Marie Rambert commented on 'the blessed poverty' in which the company existed in the early days and from which they learned so much. Referring to the tiny stage at the Mercury Theatre, where Frederick Ashton and Antony Tudor created their earliest works, she considered this to be a 'wonderful hard school for my choreographers: to try to use every inch of space to a purpose, to try to use every artist on the stage to a purpose. The artists themselves had to be absolutely sincere because the audience was so near one would feel any falsehood.'* A sure example of artistic invention born of necessity.

Areas for consideration include choreography, music and sound, design and lighting – the artistic aspects and, for most dancers, the enjoyable elements. Dealing with funding, payments, booking space for performance and rehearsals, publicity, security, insurance, front of house and other administrative arrangements are at best a labour of love, at worst a chore, or even a nightmare. Expert assistance is necessary in all specialised areas, but it is a great advantage if *you* have some knowledge of the areas, if only to be able to communicate effectively with your colleagues.

When seeking collaborators, the first problem encountered will be financial. How will you pay them, and how much will they expect? Returning to the 'grey area' between the amateur and professional worlds, the best advice is to ask around; personal recommendation from other dancers, teachers, choreographers, companies, theatres, arts centres or colleges is one of the best ways to find co-workers. You can, indirectly, get an idea of the likely fee they will want, prior to making contact. Unless you are amongst the most successful members of the dance profession, very few earn much money, so most artists will be flattered to be asked for their services, even if they are unable to help. You simply may not have sufficient funds to engage say, a costume designer and maker, *plus* a lighting designer, technician, and administrator, let alone a composer or musician. So you must decide who is absolutely essential, who you can do without, and who could act in several capacities. How you can get round such seemingly impossible limitations is the subject of this book.

At the outset, let your artistic imagination have full play, and your logical mind think through the practical areas thoroughly. It is well worth making contact with organisations which offer support to dance workers, like the National Dance Agencies, The Foundation for Community Dance and Dance UK. Addresses at the end of the book.

---

*Ballet Rambert – The First Fifty Years, BBC TV 1976

PART ONE

1. The Venue_____

There are no purpose-built theatres for dance in the way that there are theatres for the dramatic arts, concert halls for music and opera houses for opera. Even the national companies have to share performance spaces with other users. There is, as yet, no Dance House in London ... Dance needs more and better spaces. Appropriate space makes a significant impact not only on the safety and welfare of dancers, but also on the quality of experience of the audience. These needs are often poorly understood. One of the main purposes of this document is to state those needs more clearly.

Mark Foley in *Dance Spaces*

Finding a suitable place to dance is one of the biggest challenges facing a dancer or administrator. Venue managers, also, should consider the needs of any dance group they wish to book.

Dance needs space
Of all art forms, dance is the one most in need of space. This may seem like a statement of the obvious, but it is amazing how little non-dancers appreciate the amount of space needed. A 5ft 4in dancer in *arabesque* spans 1.7m–1.8m (5ft 6in–5ft 9in) from fingertip to toe tip. Multiply this by twelve, and you get the width needed for a small *corps de ballet*. Depth is another matter, as only with sufficient depth can dancers really build a series of jumps *en diagonale*, and the ceiling must be high enough for partner work with lifting involved.

In all venues the basic elements are the same, although the details may differ. There will always be:

- the performance area
- the audience area
- the backstage area
- the front-of-house area.

The shape, dimensions, atmosphere and facilities are what make the difference. You have to ensure that:

- the space is used in a way which will most enhance the dance
- the audience can see it clearly
- performers and public are as comfortable as possible.

Performance spaces for dance today include theatres, community centres, village halls, school halls, gymnasiums, art galleries, museum, open-air venues and site-specific locations. A theatre generally has a fixed layout of performance and audience areas, whereas a non-theatre venue such as a gymnasium may have a degree of flexibility regarding the layout, with the final arrangement being dictated by electrical outputs and audience entrances and exits.

In all venues, whether theatre of alternative, the dimensions of the performance space and the placement of any wings should be considered before choreographing a single movement. Studios, school halls or gymnasiums can be converted up to a point to resemble a theatre; they can work well if judiciously adapted and taken into account whilst the work is being created.

TYPES OF THEATRE

The design of theatres has been subject to fashions in architecture, with facilities onstage, backstage and front-of-house varying considerably.

However, the arrangement of performance area and audience generally falls into one of several categories: proscenium, end stage, thrust, in-the-round or arena. See diagram on page 7.

Proscenium The proscenium arch acts to separate audience and performance areas and creates most people's idea of a theatre space (which may include an orchestra pit).

End stage Here performers and audience are contained in the same space, with the stage area undefined architecturally. The audience may be level with the stage or, preferably, on raised seating, which is often erected on rostra.

Thrust stage A thrust stage has the audience on three sides, as at London's Young Vic. Dance in this space need to consider the three-sided placement of the watchers, adjusting or specially adapting the choreography so as to avoid a sideways view of essentially fronted action.

In-the-round or arena As the name suggests, the audience is on all sides, such as at London's Roundhouse. Like a thrust stage, this presents an interesting challenge to the choreographer: where and how to focus the action in relation to the surrounding public.

Traverse form The audience can be arranged on two sides. Fergus Early has exploited this form with his company Green Candle, discussed in Part Two.

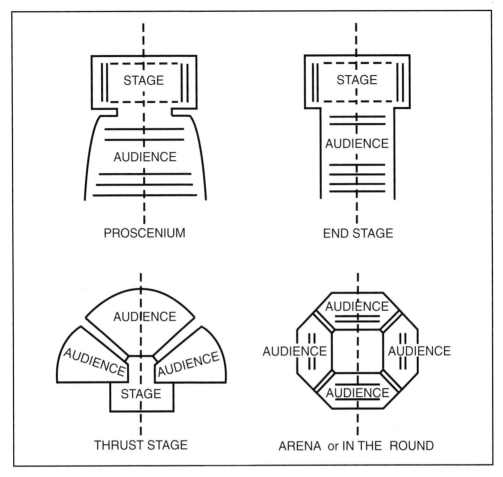

Types of theatre

Site-specific work In site-specific work, performers and audience may mingle and there may be no actual seating area, in which case the programme should not be too long, as the audience will not be able to stand for an extended period.

Opera house and large-scale theatre

The grandest of traditional proscenium theatres is the Opera House – London's Covent Garden, New York's Metropolitan – seating several thousand, specialising in stagings of opera and large-scale ballet and dance companies. Ballet companies permanently resident in such theatres are often envied, as they appear to enjoy facilities unheard of outside. Technical departments are at their disposal, including wardrobe, carpentry, scenery, properties, armoury and electrical. However, this is not always as luxurious as it appears, as a ballet company sharing an opera house often has to fit in with the opera company schedule, which takes priority. This means fewer performances than is ideal and limited stage time, because of the constantly changing repertory.

15, Gordon Street,
London WC1H 0AH
Admin: 0171-383 5976   Fax: 0171-383 4080
Ticket Office: 0171-388 8822
Technical: 0171-391 1361
General Manager: Kath Abrahams

TECHNICAL INFORMATION SHEET

SEATS	515 – 558 plus 35 standing		
	Licensed bar and Long Gallery Coffee Bar		

STAGE WIDTH	Wall to wall	79' 3"	(24.16m)
	Stage left wing		
	Stage right wing	26' 7"	(8.1m)

PROSCENIUM	Width	29' 11"	(9.12m)
	Height	24'	(7.32m)

STAGE DEPTH	Main Stage	30' 8"	(9.35m)
	+ 1st Forestage	39' 3"	(11.97m)
	(Width	8' 7"	(2.63m)
	+ 2nd Forestage	49' 2"	(14.98m)
	(Width	9' 9"	(2.97m)

STAGE HEIGHT	Stage floor to top flying dead	60'	(18.29m)
	Stage floor to underside of Fly Gallery	23'	(7.01m)
	Maximum flying width	37'	(11.28m)

STAGE RAKE   None

MACHINERY   23 double purchase counterweight sets, 3 hemp sets; separate double purchase counterweight set for house tabs, all operated from the fly floor (stage left)

CINEMA SCREEN   On counterweight sets 6 & 7.   32' x 17'   (9.7 x 5.15m)

DRESSING ROOMS	DR 1	4 artists	
	DR 2	4 artists	
	DR 3	9 artists	
	DR 4	14 artists	

The Bloomsbury Theatre is owned and funded by University College London

Printed on 100% recycled paper

FACILITIES   Crew room / green room
                    Laundry room; washing machine, tumble dryer, fridge
                    2 payphones
                    Drinks machine

PROMPT CORNER   Stage manager's desk stage left or stage right
                    Safety curtain control situated downstage right

GET-IN   Access through get-in doors (front doors)
                    Door Height   7'
                    Door Width   4'

PAINT FRAME   Electrically operated paint frame bridge complete with
                    (Available for hire)
                    Height   24'   (7.31m)
                    Width   36'   (10.97m)

PROJECTION ROOM   2 Phillips 35mm FP 20 (2kw Xenon) projectors
                    1 16mm projector
                    Full Dolby sound system

MISCELLANEOUS   Black serge drop   40' x 24'
                    1 x Black house border   36' x 10'
                    4 x Black serge legs   8' x 24'
                    4 x Black serge legs   8' x 23'
                    2 x Black borders   36' x 6'
                    2 x Black borders   36' x 8'
                    8 x Black masking flats   6' x 18'
                    2 x Black book flats   20' high
                    1 x White cyclorama   37' x 29'
                    Steinway 'D' grand piano

AUDIO-VISUAL   A full range of audio-visual equipment can also be
                    hired on behalf of the client.

See separate sheet for sound and lighting equipment

Technical information distributed by the Bloomsbury Theatre to groups wishing to make use of the theatre's facilities

Most major cities have a theatre capable of housing a large or medium-scale dance company. Generally this will be for visiting companies, which must be able to fill seats and comparatively few can be sure of doing this. Other large theatres present popular musicals featuring dance – like *Riverdance* – with which they can guarantee full houses.

Technical specifications

The technical specifications of any venue should be considered carefully before making a booking. This will describe facilities onstage, backstage and front of house. To give you an idea what a good venue for dance should offer, look at the technical specifications (pp 8–9) of London's Bloomsbury Theatre, a proscenium theatre which houses small to medium-scale dance groups as well as drama and opera productions.

Audience sightlines

The sightlines govern how visible the stage action is to the audience. Some theatres have better sightlines than others, with the most expensive seats having the best of all. Where dance is concerned, it is always desirable to be able to see the feet and floor area – considerations not so important with drama and opera. Raised seating or a raked auditorium are therefore ideal. Wherever possible, go and have a good look at a prospective venue, and imagine what your show will look like from the auditorium.

Class and rehearsal facilities

A dance group in any venue will need somewhere to practise. This may be a full hour-and-a-half class, or a shorter warm-up. The technical staff need to be aware that if the stage is the only space available, they must allow the dancers a period onstage free of technical work. Space and time for class should be discussed when making the booking. Ballet dancers generally do *barre* exercises and may bring in portable *barres* which can be set up onstage or in a rehearsal room. All professionals have experienced doing *barre* exercises in the gangway of the auditorium, holding on to a chair, or in the corridor outside the dressing room! However this is not ideal.

Adapting a non-theatre space

If necessity presents you with a non-theatre space to perform in, your first task is to check whether a public show is permitted there – you may need an entertainment licence from your local authority. This covers safety aspects for audience and performers, and includes fire regulations (all equipment, sets, props and curtains will need to be fireproof). Discuss this immediately with the venue's manager. The licence may contain specific regulations regarding exactly where you can seat the audience, how many you can accommodate, the proximity of exits in case of an evacuation and the number of gangways needed. Only after these details are finalised can you plan your layout of 'stage', 'auditorium' and 'backstage' areas.

The next consideration, if you are using stage lighting, is the amount of electrical power available and the placement of electrical outputs. These will determine where lighting and sound controls will be sited.

Entrances and exits of performers and audience should be considered, and how the dancers will cross over behind the stage area. If you are planning to hang a backcloth or legs (vertical strips of backcloth), you will need to decide where and how you will erect them. The same applies to stage lighting equipment.

Problem venues
If you find yourself in a challenging venue, take heart that your plight is shared by many dancemakers today. With patience, forethought, ingenuity and goodwill, there are ways round everything.

The tiny Mercury Theatre stage
In the early days of Ballet Rambert (now Rambert Dance Company), Ashton choreographed for Alicia Markova at the Mercury Theatre, its famous stage possessing the grand dimensions of 5.5m × 5.5m (18ft × 18ft). In *Foyer de Danse* (1932), he brilliantly utilised the stairway to the dressing room which was visible at the back of the stage. Dancers used the staircase as if it had been deliberately designed as part of the set, rather than an obstacle which could not be eliminated. Successful creativity is often the utilisation of something initially unpromising, turning its disadvantages into positive assets.

Say your performance is in a church hall or community centre, at one end of which is a small stage. If you eliminated three dancers, the stage could just about accommodate the work. However, there is no way for the dancers to cross the stage at the back. If there were room for a cyclorama (cyc), which there isn't, there would be insufficient depth onstage to allow the dancers to cross behind it. This means that entrances are limited to the same side as a dancer's last exit, or else involve a trip out of the stage area, through a door and round through whatever rooms are situated at the back. This could mean negotiating staircases, public access areas such as corridors or even a cafeteria, before the performers finally reach the entrance into the opposite wing. Imagine four dancers making this manoeuvre within a set number of musical bars, and you have a recipe for comedy, if not disaster!

Seat the audience on the stage
A possible solution might be to seat the audience on the stage, and have the performance on the larger remaining area. From a raised platform the audience's sightlines are better for viewing dance, especially if the movement involves floorwork, with a good view of the feet for ballet and tap. The greater depth of dancing area might allow an improvised cyc to be made out of screens placed along the back wall, thus providing a quick change area without the dancers having to leave the 'stage'. This set-up would benefit from a portable dance floor which, as well as providing a good surface, would delineate the stage space, enhancing the visual appearance and making a clean boundary for the action.

Bare dance area
If your work is not dependent on having wings and cyc, a totally bare dance area can work well. There have been ballets created for a proscenium stage, where masking and backcloth have deliberately been cleared, leaving the bare wall at the back of the stage visible and the lighting bars on show. This looks clean and allows extra space for the movement. A bare stage and portable floor are an effective solution to a venue where wings, backcloth and stage dimensions present problems.

Even ballet – which to many people means opera house and orchestra – can benefit from exposure in such a setting; the close proximity of the dancers may afford a new insight into the rigours of the art. The dancers are seen as real human beings instead of distant, heroic figures and the intimacy of a fine performance can be more moving when seen close at hand than when seen from up in 'the gods'.

Check the lighting
Remaining in this hypothetical hall, let's look at the lighting. There may be some lights on the stage and there may or may not be a lighting technician. As you have now moved the performing area off the stage, you may be having second thoughts, realising you will lose the lighting. Think hard: are cramped dancers preferable to a few spotlights? Check the state of these lights: who is to operate them, and are they available to rehearse the cues? Will the rehearsal cost extra for the technician's time? Unless you have a technician to focus the lights correctly and attend to all the other skilled aspects of lighting, you would be advised to scrap them altogether, and perform using auditorium and working lights.

If you do not have the resources, whether of staff, money or time, do not be over-ambitious.

Conditions to avoid
Whilst being realistic about the aesthetic considerations of the space, never accept conditions which are injurious to the performers. Health and safety for dancers are of vital importance. In the search for somewhere to perform within financial constraints, artists have often danced in halls with concrete floors, inadequate heating and ventilation, and poor backstage facilities. Such conditions lead to injury. All the research into dancers' needs and the lobbying to effect change are undermined when a group agrees to work in unacceptable circumstances. I am not suggesting that unrealistic demands are made, just that dancers take their art seriously enough to state their needs to an unenlightened outside world.

Matching company and venue
Necessity as often as choice dictates where a dance performance takes place. However, if circumstances offer you a choice of venue, take the space which most enhances your type of work. Val Bourne, Director of Dance Umbrella, says, 'It is very important to match company and venue. As well as considering whether a group will fill a theatre, the environment of the chosen space profoundly affects the work being performed. An intimate piece will fail to make an impact in a too-large space, and a formal theatre setting may destroy the spontaneity of an informal presentation; some work is actually best suited to a studio situation. Other companies will need a large space or special technical facilities.'

Type of audience
Also consider how many seats will be sold, a factor affected by the kind of audience commonly attending a venue and the type of productions generally houses there. Some towns may have seen predominantly ballet companies, with no regular audience for modern work, or vice versa. You may need to build an audience.

Building an audience
You may need to attract people who do not normally visit the theatre. Performances

in non-theatre venues often reach new audiences, with education projects, workshops and residencies playing an important part. This is one reason why companies feature education work so prominently. Be prepared not only to give your show, but to consider giving classes, workshops or open rehearsals as part of a package.

Cochrane Theatre

Theatres themselves generally have a policy regarding the type of presentations they prefer to house and dance is no exception. The Cochrane Theatre, seating 314, is a small to mid-scale proscenium theatre situated in Central London. General Manager, Teerth Chungh, explained the type of work preferred:

> We are committed to youth-based work, or work which is new, exciting and innovative in some way. Because the Cochrane is self-financing and not dependent on funding, we are in a good position to promote work with an element of risk – we do not need to make money, but can just break even, so experimental or dangerous work can be given a chance.
>
> We also feature types of dance which are generally not well represented, but are classically historic to the development of dance. Forms such as Kathak and Bharata Natyam, for example, are part of a huge dance culture not always highlighted or focused upon.
>
> We also like to give a company more focus and exposure, and create a bigger event than the one- or two-off performances which other venues offer. We have developed a close relationship with certain companies, including Union Dance, Irie! Dance Company, RJC Dance Theatre and Black Mime Theatre, all of whose work challenges the contemporary dance identity with their mix of cultures. We feature each company for a regular week's season, giving them a greater presence in London, involving schools and building up a following.
>
> Apart from the technical facilities we offer, we also have a responsibility to the artists performing. A theatre can help towards a company's development by offering a safe space and environment in which to try out new ideas, plus sympathetic and astute promotion.

ALTERNATIVE VENUES

Site-specific work

Site-specific work is also successful in bringing dance to a new public, e.g. Lea Anderson's *Opéra Sportif*, commissioned for performance in a sports hall, and Dance Umbrella's presentation in the foyer of London's Natural History Museum (1996). One New York production was seen by 50,000 people: in order to reach a new public, a myriad of free dance activities, covering all genres and styles, took place in shopping malls and arcades, culminating in an event staged on a swing bridge and timed just prior to a huge firework display!

Blitz

The annual Blitz dance festival held at London's Royal Festival Hall, is a prime example of how a venue not built for dance performances can be made to work successfully. Most of the Blitz activities take place, not in the main theatre, Queen Elizabeth Hall or Purcell Room, but in the foyer area of the Festival Hall. Generally used as an exhibition area, though originally intended as a ballroom, the space appears initially to be an unpromising one for dance performances.

Blitz's organiser Shân Maclennan points out that the festival's unique selling point is that it consists of professional and non-professional work, all styles of dance, many different kinds of performer, every type of audience. Events in 1996 included a commissioned dance piece by Charles Linehan and a day of dance for children run by DACI (Dance and the Child International). Shân Maclennan comments: 'The juxtaposition of serious contemporary dance and children's involvement is exciting'.

Technical director, Bill Deverson, described the flexibility needed for such a venture as Blitz:

> Some events use the whole space, while others use only the central area of the ballroom. This is a clear section between four pillars, laid with a dance floor, and upon which the stage lights are focused. The area cannot be totally blacked out, but we have blackout curtains along one side which can be drawn. Having to accommodate the work of so many different groups, and with a schedule allowing very little time in between each event, the technical facilities need to be very specific. Basically, the lighting rig must provide maximum effect for minimum maintenance, and the side lights must be able to be moved quickly and easily, so that the space can quickly be transformed from performance to workshop area.
>
> In addition, when planning the technical side, the fact that the Festival Hall is a listed building must also be taken into consideration. Many things are not permitted by the Department for National Heritage, and certain functions exist within the hall which cannot be changed. However, with pressures to develop the resources of the whole building, a degree of flexibility has been achieved.

A permanent trussing system is in existence in the ballroom, but this is not sufficiently strong to bear the weight of stage lights, so Bill had to erect lighting bars and stretch steel wires (catineries) between the pillars. Side lights were on easily moved stands for quick clearance after the show – as Bill says, 'Clearing cable out of the way is the worst job.' In order to make different colour washes available without spending time changing colour gels, Bill had overhead lights with automatic changes.

With the sheer number of groups appearing and lack of time available for technical rehearsals, Bill used a 24-way *manual* lighting board, pointing out that there is no time to programme cues into one which is computer operated. Bill is also able to 'feel' the movement of light as it happens with the dance, and therefore prefers to operate the equipment herself, leaving a helper to work the sound system. The Blitz sound system accommodates cassette, CD, DAT and reel-to-reel, but her advice for novice choreographers is always to have a first-class cassette version of the music. Venues vary in their sound equipment but *all* will have a cassette deck, and they are easy to operate. She also points out that reel-to-reel tapes have different speeds, and whilst all reel-to-reel machines play 7½ IPS, the better sound quality of 15 IPS is not always available.

Blitz has a grand piano permanently on hand to be wheeled wherever on the space it was needed and, with several live bands also appearing, sufficient amplification and microphones were necessary. For classes and workshops with

Alternative dance space: Ballet into the 21st Century *at Blitz '96 at the Royal Festival Hall, showing dance floor, pillars and audience area* (PHOTO: *Susan Crow*)

large groups, those leading the sessions could need radio mikes, and Bill had clip-on styles and 'headset' versions ready to accommodate the varying dance styles which teachers might demonstrate whilst wearing the mike.

One 1996 Blitz project served as an investment in the future of creativity in the ballet world, offering as part of Ballet into the 21st Century a mini course in choreography to ballet graduates, devised by Susan Crow, with workshops led by Jennifer Jackson. Susan remarked how Blitz redefined the perception of a suitable venue for ballet, which so often is synonymous with a proscenium arch theatre. 'Certain works need a traditional theatre setting, but ballet can be exciting when seen in less orthodox surroundings. Blitz also featured ballet in an independent context – a context which increasingly can provide much-needed opportunities for experimental work by ballet choreographers.'

Dance in museums, art galleries and churches
Museums, art galleries and churches can make alternative venues. Tina Cockett described a project held in the British Museum:

Indian dance does not need a theatre setting and can work well in alternative spaces, including out-of-doors and in museums and art galleries. One performance took place amongst the deities in the Hotung Gallery of the British Museum, an ideal setting for the soloist who performed her ritual front-facing the deity, and which placed the temple dance in its correct context.

Indian dance does not generally need a large space. Traditionally danced on a compacted mud surface in India, the dancers are used to a hard floor, although the characteristic stamping can only be maintained for 10–15 minutes on concrete, if injury is to be avoided. The work is always danced barefoot, and a smooth wooden sprung floor is the ideal, with or without a dance linoleum, but never on a carpet.

Dance in galleries can be choreographed round exhibits such as sculpture. Dance in churches may be part of the worship, or be enhanced by the setting. Specially created work can utilise the spatial, as well as the religious aspects: the nave, choir stalls, steps, and variety of entrances and exits can help to shape the choreography.

THEATRE TERMS AND CONVENTIONS

Do not assume that everyone knows what certain theatre terms mean. It might be your job to give newcomers information on theatre conventions, etiquette and appropriate behaviour on- and backstage. This includes:

Theatre calls Before the start of the show, the Stage Manager lets the performers know how much time there is until curtain-up. Traditionally, all those appearing in the first act (or dance) must be in the theatre 35 minutes beforehand, if not earlier. This is known as the 'half hour call' or 'the half' and is followed by 'the quarter', 'the five' and 'beginners', which is called five minutes before curtain-up to allow all performers to assemble onstage. Dancers are generally in the theatre long before 'the half' as they need to warm up as well as make up.

Stage directions Stage directions are taken from the position of a person standing onstage facing the front, auditorium or footlights. Imagine yourself in this position.

'Prompt side' or 'prompt corner' refers to the area in the wings, on your left, and is named after the place where the prompter usually stands in drama.

'Opposite prompt' or 'O.P.' is the other side, or on your right.

'Downstage' is towards the footlights.

'Upstage' is towards the backcloth.

'Stage right' and 'stage left' are taken from the same standpoint.

Listening to the Stage Manager The importance of the Stage Manager should be explained, as young people often get used to taking instructions only from their teacher. They must listen to the Stage Manager once they are onstage, in the wings or backstage.

When the instructions 'clear the stage' are heard, it means the Stage Manager, *whose word goes*, wishes the performers to leave the stage area so that technical work can take place. When in the wings, silence must be maintained, and entrance and exit areas kept clear. Dancers should never crowd into a wing to watch, chattering and blocking the performers' way or the view of Stage Manager and technicians. They should not touch, or lean on scenery or electrical items, drop rubbish or move items left out for a quick change.

The Pass Door The Pass Door in a theatre connects the front of house with the backstage area and is used by the production members only. Audiences are not allowed though the Pass Door which may have strict security features to ensure this. As well as connecting the two theatre areas, it also acts as a barrier, separating the 'make believe' world from the everyday. It is for this reason that no performer enters the audience area via the Pass Door whilst the show is in progress. Not only might this create a possible distraction to the action still continuing onstage, but the appearance of a cast member 'breaks the spell'. It reduces the mystery of the artists themselves.

Good manners The theatre is so competitive that no dancer can afford a reputation for bad manners, unreliability or casual behaviour in the workplace.

Good manners are essential in the theatre and the dressing room is no exception. Sharing a dressing room means that each person's privacy must be respected; there is often only a small amount of space for each individual and dancers quickly become adept at making themselves at home in different dressing rooms. In a very small space it is customary to vacate the dressing room when your own dance is finished, to allow another dancer to take your place. On a long tour or 'run', the behaviour of fellow cast members can make the experience a joy or a nightmare! Encourage your dancers to be a joy.

2. Flooring

Flooring is one of the most crucial staging aspects for dance. For architects and builders of dance spaces, the ideal dance floor is described in technical detail in two first-class books, Mark Foley's *Dance Spaces*, and *Space for Dance* by Leslie Armstrong and Roger Morgan, based on US requirements. Dance UK also offers a flooring factsheet based on Foley's book. These are recommended reading for *everyone* involved in dance, including tour organisers and theatre managers, and work is currently underway to create a recognised standard for dance floors in the UK.

The two prime considerations are the resiliency of the foundation, or sub-floor, and the surface.

Resilience

There are few dance movements not subject to the resilience of the floor. It affects the take-off and landing of jumps as well as falling, rolling, lifting and stamping. Muscles and joints in spine, legs and feet are subject to tremendous wear and tear, so adequate spring in the floor is vital to prevent and minimise injury. This is dependent on the floor's substructure, which is the responsibility of the architect and builder, so most dancers will have to make the best of whatever floors they encounter. Major companies have sufficient resources to take their own sprung wooden floors on tour, but they are the exception rather than the rule.

Details of the floor should be listed as part of the technical specifications, and should include information on the permanent floor and whether a dance lino is provided. However, it is prudent to visit the space beforehand and to jump, slide, fall, *pirouette*, stamp and tap around on the surface, yourself, if possible wearing the type of footwear to be used in performance.

SURFACE

A suitable surface for dance demands:

Flatness Many stages have some degree of rake. Older theatres were built with a raked stage to enhance the visibility of the performers from the audience. A raked stage profoundly affects a dancer's balance, to the extent that the ballet schools of the Bolshoi and Kirov Theatres in Russia have studios with floors built to the same rake as the stage, ensuring that the trainees develop their technique to cope with it. Compared with dancers trained on a flat floor, they can appear to centre their bodyweight further back to counteract the slope's tendency to throw the weight forward.

Dancers working on a variety of flat and raked stages make continual adjustments to their weight placement, often fully adapting only after several performances. A raked stage can present real problems to inexperienced dancers, particularly with *pointe* work and turns. It is like being at sea for several days, and then coming on to *terra firma*! For dance to work safely and effectively, a rake should be no more than 1:45.

Smoothness and evenness The surface should be smooth and even, without lumps, bumps, pits, troughs, loose boards or splinters. Check for technical and scenic items such as trapdoors, revolving stages, cables and electrical points, and for gaps and variations in level. Special flooring used for other purposes – say, an opera or play – must be investigated well before the technical rehearsal. Floorcloths must not have ridges or bubbles; textures such as artificial grass or turf, leaves or soil, must be taken into account before the choreography is set, and the designer must involve the choreographer in any decision regarding flooring. It is no good discovering during production week that the dance is made impossible by the presence of surface obstacles or textures. These can present actual dangers to the performers, as well as hindering the artistic effect.

Minimum slipperiness For most forms of dance, a slippery floor is a disaster; only ballroom dancers actively benefit from a slightly slippery surface, with barefoot work also possible if there are no splinters. Ballet companies always have a tray of rosin, which helps to prevent slipping. Occasionally even the most generous application is insufficient. Unwitting cleaners sometimes polish the floor, and this may need stripping before work can commence. This takes time and someone to do it , who will need notice and possibly payment. If stripping is not essential, washing the floor with a proprietory cleaner may suffice, but time must be allowed for it to dry before it can be danced on.

Occasionally a manager is concerned that rosin will ruin the floor, so bans its use. If you discover this ahead of time, negotiate other options, including a different venue. If it is ideal in every other respect, then suggest hiring or borrowing a portable linoleum. Remember, dance always needs a decent floor; if the venue is keen to attract dance performances, it should offer appropriate facilities. Some places are simply not aware of the needs of dance and you may be the first person to open the eyes of the managers.

Another solution might be to dance barefoot, which would give a different effect, but some pieces work surprisingly well when taken off *pointe* into flat shoes, or from flat shoes to bare feet.

When different dance disciplines are included within a single show, a sprung, non-slippery smooth wooden floor will work for most items, with linoleum on top as an option. Tap needs a floor which allows the full sound of the metallic taps, often deadened by lino. A wooden floor suitable for tap and *pointe* work, but too splintery for bare feet, may work if the barefoot dancers wear flesh-coloured flat shoes which give the illusion of bare feet, whilst protecting the toes.

Portable dance floors

If resources allow, you may be wise to acquire a portable linoleum dance floor. Some portable floors contain a small degree of helpful 'spring'. Dance floor specialists make portable floors to suit individual budgets and requirements. These are laid in strips, taped down, then allowed to 'settle' for a few hours. Floorwork and *pointe* work are comfortable on linoleum, and there are special floors available for tap, so the value of owning a floor can be worth the initial expense. Remember that rolls of linoleum are heavy, needing transport and someone to carry and to lay them.

Your surface will need maintaining, whether this means just sweeping over between shows or an occasional wash. A clean floor is important for look and safety, as bits of costume, including sequins, can fall off and cut bare feet. Equally important are floor surfaces in the wings and adjacent rooms, also on stairs and in corridors leading to the stage. Care of the stage is generally the job of the Stage Manager, but if you do not have one, then it may be up to YOU!

3. Choreography

The choreographer is such a key figure in all dance productions, that his role must be understood and his skills fully appreciated, before a truly successful staging can take place. Successful staging is the effective translation of the artistic aims of choreographer, composer and designer into theatrical reality. The artistic intention of the choreographer is a major, possibly the most crucial factor, in the shape which the final production will take.

With the diversity of today's dance activity, how should you proceed with your own creative ideas? Choreography is a vast subject, so I have concentrated here on three aspects, the history, the craft and the process. These areas overlap in the creation of a work: historical examples act as models, the craft helps to shape the choreography and the process is governed by outside influences such as time and money. In practice they all work together, but I have separated them, here, to concentrate on specific points.

HISTORY

You may have seen a dance performance which excited you, and which acts to some extent as a model, so I will look briefly at the work of several creators who have influenced today's choreographers: Marius Petipa and Lev Ivanov, Michel Fokine, George Balanchine, Frederick Ashton, Martha Graham and Merce Cunningham.

As well as creating some of the most celebrated works of the last 150 years, each has had a significant influence on the development of dance staging, and all have enjoyed distinguished associations with composers and designers. Musical partnerships have brought together Petipa and Ivanov with Pyotr Tchaikovsky in *Swan Lake* and *The Nutcracker*, Balanchine and Igor Stravinsky in *Apollo*, Cunningham and John Cage in *Fielding Sixes*. Design collaborations engaged Fokine and Leon Bakst in *Schéhérazade* and Fokine and Alexander Benois in *Petrouchka*; and Ashton and Sophie Fedorovitch in *Symphonic Variations*.

Choreographer/composer/designer collaborations involve Graham and Aaron Copland and Isamu Noguchi to produce *Appalachian Spring*.

The sound and look of these works have been as important as the movement. The type of theatres or other venues for which the pieces were created has also been significant. At each point in the development of ballet and modern dance a specific set of theatrical values and performance locations has been evident.

Petipa created for the grand opera house, and Mary Clarke and Clement Crisp in *Making a Ballet* describe the opportunities and limitations which this provided:

> From 1862 to 1903, he (Petipa) produced a series of ballets *à grand spectacle* to enshrine the massive forces and ever developing technical skill of the Russian

dancers ... Petipa's procedure in creating his big ballets – three and four act spectacles which lasted a whole evening and were designed to titillate the taste of his Court audience – seems to have been codified early on. Having chosen his theme, which in many cases would have been suggested by contemporary events, he drafted a very clear libretto breaking up the action into scenes and actual numbers, and it is from this detailed libretto that he started work. The writing of the score was entrusted to that remarkable figure, the 'official' composer of ballet music to the theatre – two incumbents of the position during Petipa's time were Pugni and Minkus – and they were required to furnish precisely measured numbers: processions, ballabili, polkas, waltzes, variations, *pas de deux*, whose dramatic point was rarely considered in the writing.

...There was no more sense in the design. Sets were created to rigid formulae: they were to be provided by the paint shops and official scenic artists to the theatre who could devise temples or palaces or forest scenes with no more thought than went in to the creation of the score. Costume followed certain rigid rules: the ballerina must wear pink toe-shoes and a tutu. If the ballet were Egyptian her skirt might have some Egyptian decoration; were it Greek, a border of the key pattern would suffice.

In 1909, Serge Diaghilev founded the Ballets Russes, regenerating the art form after the decline of the Imperial Ballet. Michel Fokine pioneered new ways of choreographing and collaborating; his choreographic reforms brought a renewed sense of reality to classical conventions, a freedom of movement inspired by the work of Isadora Duncan, and greater equality between dance, music and design.

Diaghilev invited modern painters, including Pablo Picasso, to design for the Ballets Russes and commissioned serious composers like Stravinsky and others who might otherwise have scorned to write music for ballet. Stagings were still spectacular – but instead of relying on the predictable 'in house' creations of the old opera houses, eminent easel painters took to the stage. As well as Picasso, Natalia Goncharova, André Derain, Henri Matisse and Joan Miro all designed for the Ballets Russes. Claude Debussy, Francis Poulenc and Erik Satie composed scores.

Balanchine took America by storm in the 1930s, founding the New York City Ballet and a whole new style. Renowned for his collaborations with Stravinsky, he created notable ballets with designs by artists such as Christian Bérard and Eugene Berman, but is perhaps best known for his plotless, neoclassical works where the movement was stripped bare of anything superfluous, including costumes and sets. He adapted the classicism of his Imperial Russian background to the physique and temperament of the American dancers, and incorporated influences from jazz culture. In a distinctive new look based on dancers' practice-dress for costume, and a bare and uncluttered stage, stage lighting began to take on an increasingly important role. Lighting designer Jean Rosenthal worked with Balanchine and Graham in the 1930s and 1940s and dance lighting took on a new lease of life.

In Britain, Rambert and de Valois founded companies which became Ballet Rambert (now Rambert Dance Company) and The Royal Ballet. Frederick Ashton, Antony Tudor and Kenneth MacMillan emerged as world-class choreographers. They were crucial to the careers of Margot Fonteyn, Lynn Seymour, Antoinette Sibley and Anthony Dowell, and their works have influenced many British choreographers working today.

In America, Graham rejected ballet and evolved her own movement forms to express man's 'inner landscape', based on the contraction and release of breathing. She brought about further innovations in music and design, exploiting stage constructions by Isamu Noguchi which appeared as sculptured objects integral to the dance, and demanded new ways of lighting. Noguchi's sculptures were made in modern materials such as chrome and gave a three-dimensional look, frequently echoing the symbolism in Graham's choreography. Her work was highly theatrical, her costumes using clinging, stretch fabrics to reveal the movements' sculptural qualities, with voluminous skirts and cloaks sometimes covering a substantial area of the stage. She treated themes such as Greek mythology and she was committed to creating a distinctively American art form, commissioning American composers like Aaron Copland.

Cunningham began as a dancer with Graham, but rejected her expressionistic aims, and turned his choreographic vision towards movement for its own sake. His work featured radical collaborations with composer John Cage, using aleatory (chance) techniques to create both movement and music. These were created independently of each other, sometimes coming together only at the first performance. Cunningham revolutionised many aspects of the traditional notions of creating a ballet. He explored the rhythm, dynamics and phrasing naturally inherent in movement, without the influence of accompaniment, and also did away with the centralisation of the stage action. His company danced in hitherto unexplored venues for dance such as gymnasiums and he coined a new term, 'Events', to describe the performances.

In the 1960s, American choreographers like Yvonne Rainer were concerned with finding alternatives to traditional concepts of dance and were influenced by the minimalist movement in art. Rigid technique was rejected in favour of natural, everyday movement. They rejected traditional theatre venues, seeking alternatives not only in bricks and mortar, but also in the relationship between audience and performer. Amongst possibilities which emerged were dance performed on a roof, and dance performed for the dancer alone, without an audience. If you are influenced by ideas like these, then the very notion of 'staging' dance may be alien, but I would guess that a degree of planning must go into a performance of this type, even if 'performance' is not a favoured term.

Modern dance has seen the growth of a whole movement of independent creators working in Europe and Australia as well as in the USA. They have explored diverse areas, including everyday, pedestrian movement, contact improvisation, release work and 'soft' martial arts like tai chi and aikido. It is against this background that choreographers of today are working.

With the variety of dance activities being currently staged, and the many different performance spaces available through choice or necessity, I think it wise to reflect on the appropriate matching of genre to venue.

THE CRAFT OF CHOREOGRAPHY

Like music, choreography exists in time, and like painting and sculpture, it exists in space. Time and space underly all aspects of the choreographic craft. The craft gives shape, clarity and interest to the movements. It helps the choreographer to express his ideas and enables the audience to understand them. Everyone is familiar with human movement and can understand and appreciate it on an everyday level. Human movement is the choreographer's material, and he fashions it into an artistic statement. It is beyond the scope of this book to explore choreographic craft in depth, and there are several good books on the subject mentioned in the bibliography.

However, it is important to remember the time and space aspects. Like music, dance continues for a certain length of time, unlike painting and sculpture where the 'statement' is made once. A painting doesn't have to last ten minutes. A dance has to make 'statements' clearly and interestingly for ten minutes. A choreographer must develop his movement material as a composer develops musical ideas, and he must be able to sustain interest and invention over a period of time. Appropriate and effective movement motifs or themes must be developed logically into a coherent shape with a beginning , middle and end. The ideas should unfold organically with highlights and climaxes arising naturally.

Use of space

The visual aspect of the craft involves the design and effect of movement patterns which, in staging terms, include the appropriate use of the performance space. Before starting to choreograph, you should make an exhaustive exploration of your performance space, and assess how best to utilise its advantages and minimise its weak points.

Dance itself contains powerful design elements; it has appropriately been called 'moving sculpture'. The performance space must enhance this aspect. Its dimensions, including the height of the ceiling, the position of entrances and exits, and the audience's sightlines must be taken into consideration. Similarly, it is important that venue managers understand what the use of space means from the artistic point of view and do not have unrealistic expectations.

Designs in space Design in movement occurs in space, as in a static body position or shape. Most people can understand and recognise space designs.

Designs in time Design also occurs in time, as in the shape of a movement-phrase. A phrase consists of a series of space-designs which develop from one to another, tracing patterns in the air and on the floor. Time designs, or moving shapes and patterns, are less easy to spot and a choreographer must learn to develop his 'eye' in order to grasp them.

Some dance styles and choreographers lay particular emphasis on the individual dancer's line. Others may focus more on the shape made by a series of movements. The stage space can be seen as a three-dimensional canvas, with movements into the air, onto and across the floor making space designs and adding variety and contrast. Space designs exist vertically and horizontally, and a good dance will explore all possibilities. As well as their linear aspects, vertical and horizontal planes in space can also have dramatic possibilities; movements reaching upwards, for example, may suggest aspiration, or those towards the floor weariness or resignation.

Symmetry and asymmetry It is also important to understand the effects of symmetry and asymmetry. Symmetry has evenly balanced proportions, equal on both sides, e.g. a single body-shape has left and right sides identical, or four dancers

Pepsi Bethel rehearses with Warren Heyes of the Jiving Lindy Hoppers (PHOTO: © 1986 Paul Armstrong)

grouped two and two equidistant from the centre. Symmetrical designs, whether in space (static) or time (moving) tend to suggest evenness and calm. Overuse of symmetry is predictable and dull. Asymmetrical designs, with uneven proportions, are stimulating and unpredictable, and are therefore more exciting to the watcher, e.g. a single body-shape with left and right sides differing, or four dancers grouped three together and one separate.

Floor patterns and group shapes Symmetry and asymmetry need to be understood in the deployment of a number of dancers, in their floor patterns and group shapes.

If you are working with a large number of dancers, your floor patterns and group shapes need to be clearly worked out in advance, so that rehearsals do not become chaotic. Many folk dances have traditionally used large groups in fascinating space designs; aspiring choreographers would gain from observing or learning such forms.

Formal patterning and groups appear in the classical ballets, like the *corps de ballet* of swans in Act Two of *Swan Lake,* moving in endless variations of lines, files, circles, diagonals and S-shapes, with the V-shape suggestive of the flock of swans in flight. Balanchine created a wealth of imaginative configurations in *Serenade* (1937) with a more modern use of the ballet vocabulary.

Merce Cunningham revolutionised the traditional notion that the centre of the action is in the centre of the stage. In his works, the centre of the action can be anywhere on the stage and, indeed, may have several centres focused simultaneously.

Using numbers with artistry A large number of dancers does not necessarily enhance a work. The use of space is equally as important in a solo or small group. Even with a large cast, it can be tedious if the space is constantly filled with bodies. Numbers should be used with artistry, varying the designs that can be made with many or few dancers.

Amount of space available The amount of space available will crucially affect the end result. On a small stage, six dancers look like a lot, and can even suggest a crowd; on an enormous stage, a single child can look lost; too many dancers make the space look cluttered. The relative width or depth of a stage may necessitate specific respacing of patterns – making larger, smaller, 'flattening out' or 'sharpening' the angles of diagonal lines. Choreographically, extra steps may be needed to expand a work onto a very large space, as well as travelling out the existing ones.

In venues with limited wing space or awkward entrances and exits, the logistics of getting dancers on and offstage should be taken into account. If there is only a small door available, and this cannot be masked from the audience, exits can result in an ungainly queue or, worse, a pile-up of dancers waiting to get off. Dancers may also be waiting to get onstage. As well as being a distraction, this could cause injury if large numbers were involved.

Room must also be allowed for scenery and sets (whether flats and free-standing, or gauzes and cloths), furniture, stage sculpture and props. Dancers must not collide with each other or with a piece of scenery. There have, of course, been innumerable instances where something has gone wrong relative to the space available and to the placing of dancers or scenery. These range from the hilarious to the downright dangerous.

THE CHOREOGRAPHIC PROCESS

The choreographic process consists of various stages before a work reaches its first performance. It is concerned with outside factors which are predetermined and with which the choreographer must deal. It also gives an idea of the order in which things happen, and the planning schedules of collaborators.

The commission and idea
Either the commission, or the artistic idea for a dance may come first. An idea for a dance may be in the choreographer's mind for years before the opportunity arises actually to put it on. Alternatively, the commission may be the thing which sparks off a new dance.

Once you know that a piece is actually to happen, with a deadline, first night and (hopefully) a fee, consider your general aims and those of the producer.

General aims
- are you choreographing a dance or a work?
- in what type of programme will the finished piece appear?
- how long will your choreography be?

- what style of movement will you use?
- who are the dancers?
- how many dancers?
- how much time do you have?
- what is the budget?

These considerations will give an overall impression, style and starting point for the actual choreography. Each provides a limit or boundary within which the work will take shape and will dictate certain features. Limitations are often thought to be obstacles to creativity, whereas in fact they help to narrow down options and to focus the direction a work will take.

A dance or a work? The main difference between a dance and a work is its length. Consider a dance to last up to eight minutes and a work to be longer. Some works consist of a series of individual dances, each with a clear beginning and end. In others, the movement develops so that each part flows continuously into the next without a 'break'. Many works include both types of structure.

Type of programme Are you choreographing:

- a work which will appear in a programme with pieces by other choreographers?
- an entire show?

If the former, you may be required to create a piece specifically to fit in with other works.

'OPENERS' This might be an 'opener', to go at the beginning of the programme. Openers tend to be relatively undemanding for the audience, particularly if they are to be followed by a strong dramatic or otherwise challenging work. The audience will be settling down in their seats, and bear in mind the importance of first impressions.

Possibilities include plotless pure-dance works which are easy on the eye, or ballets with gentle humour or subtle drama. The choreographer must remember that the opener will include the dancers' first appearance onstage, and it may be unwise to ask them to launch immediately into extremely vigorous, technically demanding movement, or into high drama. They, as well as the audience, need a little time to warm up.

WORKS PLACED IN THE MIDDLE OF A PROGRAMME A centrally placed ballet will be the focus of the evening and will tend to have more 'weight'. It could be a première, or its importance could be in terms of subject matter, innovation or historical significance. Or it could be a vehicle for the talents of a leading dancer or guest artist.

FINAL WORKS IN A PROGRAMME The final work in a programme could be something thought-provoking, or an exhilarating 'grand finale' style piece, which sends the audience away on a high. Or it might contain high-risk technical virtuosity and have the watchers on the edge of their seats. If it is preceded by a powerful, famous or important middle ballet, a low-key work can round off the evening quietly, on the principle that it can be difficult to follow a masterpiece. It is certainly unwise to try to compete.

The positioning of works in a programme needs skilled judgement and the understanding of the desired effect of each item. Other staging features also come into play, such as whether a scene change from one work to another can be completed in a fifteen-minute interval, and whether the dancers have sufficient time to do a full hair and make-up change.

Find out what else is being shown, and where your piece fits in. If you are familiar with your companion pieces, you may like to offer a contrast. Is there anything lacking which you could provide? For example, there might be two pieces containing fast, athletic movement and modern music, so you might decide to choreograph a gentler, slower work using classical music. If your companion pieces use taped sound, consider live music. If they use a large cast, you might try a trio. If they are serious in mood, you might like to add wit and humour. Some shows include a variety of dance styles, so you might be creating the only dance which represents, say, tap.

How long? The duration of a piece has great bearing on how it will be approached.

SOLOS AND DUETS Works which use fewer dancers tend to be shorter than those with a large cast. A single dance, especially if it is a solo, can be as short as two minutes. A classical solo like one of the fairy variations from the Prologue of *The Sleeping Beauty* may last only a minute. Classical ballet solos demand tremendous precision, stamina and artistry, which are hard for a soloist to sustain for a long period. So a solo dance should never be too long. Likewise a duet.

THREE DANCERS OR MORE Three or more dancers can sustain much greater length.

Once you have discovered the length of the choreography required, ask yourself just how long you can sustain in terms of interest and invention. Doris Humphrey said 'All dances are too long'. No-one likes to admit that maybe ten minutes could usefully be cut out of their work, but it does help to leave the audience wanting more, rather than wondering when the interval will arrive. Novice choreographers would be well advised to start with five minutes or so, gradually building on this as they become more experienced. Longer does not necessarily mean better – Fokine's *The Dying Swan* is only a couple of minutes long, yet is one of the most famous dances of all time.

A dance should be long enough to create its effect and engage the audience's interest. It should allow the organic development of movement and, possibly, dramatic ideas. It should have a beginning, middle and end. A theme, whether stated in pure movement terms or as a dramatic situation, should be developed clearly and logically. It should also be imaginative. Structure is important, but is primarily a framework for the artist's imagination.

WAYS OF EXTENDING LENGTH If you are specifically requested to create a piece longer than you feel you can sustain, there are choreographic devices which subtly extend a work's length. Repetition of movement material is the most obvious possibility, but beware that it does not become tedious. The use of a musical form like an 'A.B.A.' or variant, allows the *reprise* of the opening section at the end of a work, without the necessity of inventing totally new movement. Beginnings and endings that use moments of silence, before and after the music or sound, can also extend a piece and allow sustained entrances and exits by the dancers. These could be done in canon, another device which can be used to create length.

CHOREOGRAPHING AN ENTIRE SHOW Choreographing an entire performance demands skill and stamina, as well as considerable organisational skills! Familiarity with a variety of dance styles is invaluable, whether you are creating one long work, or a number of separate short works. Variety and contrast in movement and programming are always needed to keep the audience's interest. These can be achieved by:

- varying the number of dancers onstage, both in separate dances and in longer sections
- changing the speed and pulse in the movement
- creating dynamic contrasts
- alternating pure dance with dramatic sections
- utilising different dance styles if you and your dancers have the skills.

Interest can also be achieved through musical and design elements.

LENGTH OF REHEARSAL PERIOD Obviously, the rehearsal period for the creation of an entire programme, will be longer than that needed for a five minute dance or 'number'. If you are working for someone else, they must understand the logistics of:

- getting the cast together
- creating and teaching the choreography
- rehearsing it.

The sheer number of people involved, particularly in a school show with children or students, requires organisation on a major scale. Non-dancers often fail to realise that creating, teaching and rehearsing a piece of choreography are three separate processes, although they may overlap and take place within a single session.

Movement style The overall style may fall into one of several categories:

- Works which are based on a technique and seek to exploit its possibilities. These include:
  ballet
  modern dance, spanning a variety of individual techniques
  jazz dance, which may include tap
  some ethnic forms such as South Asian Bharata Natyam.
- Works not based on a technique, including:
  Experimental works where the aim of the choreographer is to challenge accepted models.
  Those in which the movement style evolves predominantly from an idea or theme. Many dances combine both technical and non-technical aspects.

Who are your dancers, how many, and how much time do you have? These three factors are always connected in planning your choreography. Plenty of rehearsal time means you can experiment, and work intensively on detail and interpretation. The real world does not usually allow you either the dancers or the amount of time you would like. Assess what is possible in the circumstances.

Your dancers' abilities determine much of your working method and choreographic style. A good choreographer will exploit and enhance his dancers, at whatever level they present themselves.

The first consideration is how to use your time to best advantage. Given how long it actually takes to create, teach and rehearse a dance, assess carefully how ambitious you can afford to be. If your dancers are new to your style, or are inexperienced in learning and retaining movement, don't get carried away with grandiose ideas of what they can do or what you can achieve.

The musical *Stepping Out*, (the film version of which can be rented from your video shop) follows the struggles of an adult amateur tap class, as their valiant teacher tries to create a dance routine on them for a show. It hilariously and poignantly depicts exactly how much work goes into even the briefest of dances. The tap class members' lack of experience means that even the simplest sequence has to be continually scaled down by the teacher for her to get the job done at all. The dancers are earnest and willing, the teacher determined and compassionate – the uphill slog is just the way of all choreography! Whoever you are.

Only experience allows a choreographer to know broadly what will work in a given situation. There are some basic ground rules. Here are a few:

- a large cast takes longer, as there are more people to get right;
- everything takes longer than anticipated;
- allow for injuries, illness and missed rehearsals;
- allow for dancers, especially children, forgetting what they learned last rehearsal;
- allow for the drop in enthusiasm once the novelty has worn off;
- remember your dancers' inner performance, as well as their outer;
- don't over-rehearse;
- gauge whether a technical challenge will make an individual dancer blossom or shrivel;
- likewise an artistic or interpretive challenge;
- work backwards from the last studio rehearsal when calculating how much you need to accomplish in each session.

Most dancers are keyed up and excited at the prospect of learning a new dance for a show. Thank goodness they are! Their muscles will get sore and they may be sacrificing their social life to take part. Experienced dancers will want a challenge and may very much want a good role. Newcomers may want to learn the ropes unobtrusively and not be put on the spot or singled out for anything too demanding.

Keep the movements within the dancers' abilities, unless you really have the time to stretch them.

Non-professionals usually need all their abilities just to cope with learning and performing, so avoid unrealistic challenges. These may expose a dancer's weaknesses, and the choreographer will be judged inadequate for not allowing them to shine in an easier role.

Allowing dancers to shine demands skill and judgement. It requires acute observation of the dancers' physical and artistic strong points. A good choreographer will spot hidden dramatic talents, a good jump, a coltish innocence, a promising partnership, expressive hands, a rapt involvement, a bolshie personality, a commanding walk, a good stage face, a quick learner, a whinger, four dancers the same height, musicality, the ability to improvise, manly and womanly dancers amongst boys and girls. And so on.

Observing and assessing dancers allow you to begin to cast them and to devise movements which will suit their abilities. One of the advantages of creating, rather than reviving or restaging a work, is that you can create on the dancers you have, rather than trying to fit a new dancer into a role created for someone else. It also offers the chance to make new movement.

The choreographer's material is a living human being. This is its joy and challenge.

The budget The budget affects the number and type of dancers you use, and how much rehearsal time is available. The costs of studio hire and payment for you and the dancers will be considerable. You will need to work within limits. However, if totally unrealistic suggestions are made, or you are concerned about any aspect of the money side, discuss them with someone in charge, as soon as possible. Don't expect that problems will vanish by magic. The longer you put off facing a potentially negative situation, the worse it becomes. By the same token, you also must not make unrealistic demands, whether these concern time, money, effects or whatever. Sufficient and effective communication between choreographer and management, at the outset, will prevent nasty shocks from occurring later on. 'I thought you said I had more time, more dancers, more costumes, more leeway, etc. etc.' or 'How do you expect me to finish such and such when you didn't tell me so and so?' are all preventable by communication. And more communication. And more. Throughout the creative period.

Preparation period

Once you know your dancers, length of the rehearsal period and budget, it is time to get down to the nitty-gritty of creating.

An important part of the process is the choreographer's preparation before entering the studio for the first rehearsal. It is when the choreographer dreams about the dance, even feels passionately about it.

Subject matter and source material will be considered, and movement ideas experimented with privately. Out of this preparation period will emerge ideas for the general structure of the piece and decisions on working method.

Let's say the commission is a work with children from a dance school. Because of time and money available, you may decide to create a suite of short, individual dances. This may be the best option if the children's availability is dictated by the times of their normal dance lessons. Rehearsals are only possible in individual class groups, so creating a piece mixing dancers from two groups would not work. Keeping each dance self-contained makes the project manageable. Musically, too, it may be easier, and stylistically more satisfying, to find a series of short individual pieces by a single composer.

A 'story ballet' may need the leading characters to be available to rehearse with all the groups. The demands on children from schoolwork and families can make this impossible. There are, however, groups committed to dance to the exclusion of all

Children try out fan movements (PHOTO: *Martin Meyer*)

else, and these will allow much more scope. Aim for the most happy experience for all concerned.

With children, decide whether the group will respond better to a pattern of familiar steps or to something freer, which may involve the children's own ideas.

The former works well where the children participate in technically based dance classes, and are therefore keen to show off latest steps and skills. They will be thrilled to use their latest movements in dances with simple, formal patterns and a touch of character.

Children who have more creatively based dance lessons may enjoy making up their own movements. So you might make an overall 'sequence plan' and give the children stimulating themes upon which to create their own short movement-bites.

Music and design
The preparation period is also when the choreographer will make decisions about the music and sound, and, possibly, design. These are big subjects, and are covered in the next chapters.

Casting
Casting may include finding the dancers, as well as deciding who is to dance which part. This will mean setting up an audition. Auditions take several forms.

- An 'open' audition. Place an advertisement in the press inviting interested dancers to the studio at a specified time. Details of the production should be put in the advertisement, plus dates of rehearsals, and any specifications regarding the type of dancers you are looking for. These include gender, height, age range and special skills required, such as *pointe* work, aerial skills, street dance, physical theatre, etc. If you do not specify *pointe* work or singing, the dancers will not bring *pointe* shoes or a song, so avoid wasting time by being specific

- Inviting dancers you already know or who have been recommended, to audition.
- Holding an audition within a company or school.

At the audition

Auditions should be held sensitively and efficiently. They are always nerve-wracking but should not be humiliating. Those running the audition hold all the trump cards, so make sure your dancers feel as comfortable as possible.

- Be clear about what the audition procedure is to be. Will it be a class followed by trying out some of the choreographer's ideas?
- Will you ask the dancers to improvise?
- Should the dancers prepare something beforehand?
- Will there be partner-work?
- Will you require extra skills, such as singing or acting?

Tell the dancers as much as possible at the start of the audition. If you think there may be long waits, warn them. Above all, remember what it feels like to audition. Recall your own good and bad audition experiences and take from the best.

STUDYING CHOREOGRAPHY ON VIDEO

Greater understanding of how aspects of choreography work in practice can be gained from good dance productions. If geography and finances make seeing live work difficult, consider investing in some videos. Here are several available commercially, which illustrate points made in the book (Suppliers at the end).

- Several different productions are available of the nineteenth-century classics and of works by Fokine.
- *The Dream* by Frederick Ashton for The Royal Ballet, with music by Mendelssohn and designs by David Walker, is an excellent example of a ballet which exploits the classical vocabulary to tell a story and to create exquisite pure dance episodes. Compare the development of movement ideas in diverse episodes such as the Rustics' entry and dance, the solo of Bottom as the ass, the final *pas de deux* between Oberon and Titania and the *corps de ballet* of fairies.
- *Sergeant Early's Dream* by Christopher Bruce for Rambert Dance Company, designed by Walter Nobbe, is a suite of dances to folk songs.
- *Changing Steps* by Merce Cunningham, music by John Cage, shows Cunningham's characteristic approach to choreography, music and design.
- *Soda Lake* by Richard Alston, sculpture by Nigel Hall, and danced in silence, illustrates the power of movement independent of accompaniment, and the effectiveness of sculpture as a design element.
- *Enter Achilles*, created collaboratively by Lloyd Newson and the dancers for DV8 Physical Theatre, with music by Adrian Johnston and designs by Andrew MacNeil.

- *The Road Home*, choreographed by Fergus Early for Green Candle Dance Company, with music by Sally Davies and designs by Craig Givens, is discussed in Part Two.
- *Body as Site* by Rosemary Butcher, filmed in performance at Guildford Cathedral, shows the possibilities of dance in a non-theatre setting.

THE BUSINESS SIDE

Despite their important role, choreographers are not always accorded the status and recognition they deserve, often working in an uncertain area regarding conditions and rights.

Always investigate the business side of any arrangement as carefully as the artistic side. Negotiating a contract is often a terrifying prospect, choreographers being only too thankful someone has given them a chance.

If you are in doubt about a fee, or feel you are being underpaid, you will need to assess whether a management is exploiting your skills, or simply and genuinely does not have much, or any, money. Ask around; it is usually possible to get some idea of a manager's reputation.

To help draw attention to needs of choreographers and to offer guidance to aspirants in the absence of a clear career structure, international choreologist Ann Whitley has written *Look Before You Leap: An Advice and Rights Guide for Choreographers* (Dance UK).

4. Music and Sound

Anyone not regularly involved with dance may not appreciate the huge variety of dance/music partnerships that abound today, nor understand the importance of precise sound cues, the placing of musicians and the quality of sound reproduction.

MUSIC AND SOUND FOR CHOREOGRAPHY

According to the choreographer's working methods, musical requirements vary enormously. Some choreographers are inspired by a particular composition and some have an idea for a work for which they then seek appropriate music. Others use the rhythms and textures of a piece as a stimulus for movement, then subsequently perform the finished dance to something totally different. Some choreographers collaborate with a composer in creating new music. Others create their own sound score. The one factor which most pieces of music suitable for choreography have in common is that they are not too long. The eye is faster than the ear, so movement is grasped and absorbed more quickly than sound. A choreographer's main concerns are:

- where to find suitable music
- what to look for
- how the music/sound will be used with the movement.

It is vital for a choreographer to listen to all types of music. The more familiar he is with different styles of music, the more he will have to choose from when he needs to find a piece for a work. A knowledge of musical sources suitable for choreography is usually built up over time.

Types of music and sound
When choosing music for a work, consider whether you are drawn to a particular style: classical, rock, folk, jazz, etc. Do you want a full sound, with lots of instruments? Or a solo instrument, such as guitar, harmonica, harpsichord, saxophone, etc.? Do you want a flavour of a particular country, such as Latin America, Scotland, Israel, India? Do you want to pinpoint a particular era, such as the reign of Elizabeth I, or the 1940s and wartime? If so, listen to music of your chosen country or period.

Early music can be an evocative partner for movement. Listen to the mystical power of Gregorian chant, the rhythmic lyricism of madrigals and part-songs, and the haunting sounds of the lute, crumhorn and sackbut.

Baroque music contains many works with comparatively short sections within a longer whole, in a variety of moods and tempi. Some suites comprise movements based on dance styles: the Cello Suites of J. S. Bach include minuets, gigues, sarabandes, courantes, gavottes and allemandes. The clear structures, orderly beat and graceful melodies have a formality which makes an excellent partner for dance, as do works by classical composers like Mozart or Schubert.

Romantic music has been popular with ballet choreographers. Many comparatively short pieces are full of passion and atmosphere. Rhythmically and structurally they are often rich in imagination and development, and there are many works for solo piano.

Impressionist music contains pieces of great atmosphere, tonal interest and a more 'modern' sound. There are evocative orchestral works and solo instrumental pieces.

Twentieth-century music contains many works which make exciting partners for dance. Mainstream music largely uses traditional instruments, rather than electronic and other experimental sounds. Experimental music may use traditional instruments or electronic sounds. Modern minimalist music is effective in offering a background, whilst also containing rhythmic and textural interest which can be reflected in the movement. Once the interest of post-modern choreographers, who explored minimalism in choreography, minimalist composers like Steve Reich are becoming increasingly popular with mainstream dance makers.

Jazz and blues have been very popular for social dance forms and tap dance.

Popular music has been part of many dance works. Kenneth MacMillan's *Elite Syncopations* (1974) used Scott Joplin's popular music of the 1920s, and *Java* (1983) by Richard Alston used The Inkspots' popular music of the 1940s. Christopher Bruce's *Rooster* (1991) was a smash hit to 1960s' music by the Rolling Stones. However, music like this can trap unwary choreographers. The latest chart hits appeal to young choreographers and they do not always question whether the music is helpful. Pop music often contains long stretches of predictable and repetitious rhythms, and may contain little structural development. Only a skilled choreographer can make them work. Monotonous musical passages must be broken by strongly rhythmic and dynamic movement, and by consciously going against or through the beat. Other good choreography to popular music can be found in musicals. Local video shops stock *West Side Story, The King and I, Oklahoma!* and *Seven Brides for Seven Brothers*, the first two choreographed by Jerome Robbins, the others by Agnes de Mille and Michael Kidd respectively. The films of Fred Astaire are classics. More recently, *Grease, Tap* and *Riverdance* have used rock and roll, tap and Irish dancing, making their impact through the skilled and original use of the movement in terms of structure, rhythm, dynamics and the use of space. In *Riverdance*, unison dancing is featured, which could become predictable, but the use of mass, a large number of dancers all working exactly in sync. (offset by brilliant bursts from the soloists), keeps the excitement high.

Folk songs can also be tricky music for choreography – they are often repetitious. However, there are some notably successful ballets to folk songs, including

Christopher Bruce's *Sergeant Early's Dream*. Bruce shows perfectly how choreographic craft can be used to offset the repetitiousness. The movements are derived from ballet, modern dance and folk steps. The dancers have characters and reflect the stories told in the songs. In a very slow love song, he picks out rhythmic undercurrents in the choreography. The turbulent passion of the love duet is expressed through strong, dramatic movement, with abrupt changes of dynamics. Spatially, Bruce uses lifts and floor work to give interest and contrast. At no point is he dominated by the long phrases and insistent rhythms of the music. Instead of merely reflecting these aspects, he complements them in the movement.

World music from different cultures offers a great variety of sounds and rhythms and its very unfamiliarity makes an impact theatrically. Examples include Balinese gamelan music, Japanese kodo drumming and African traditional.

Breath, voice, speech, song
Many dance works have used breath, voice, speech or song, ranging from Tudor's *Dark Elegies* (1937) with Mahler's song cycle *Kindertotenlieder*, to Richard Alston's *Rainbow Bandit* (1974) with layered patterns made by words. If a choreographer chooses to work with words, whether spoken or sung, he must decide how he is going to deal with them. Unless the words are deliberately unintelligible, the audience will be subconsciously listening to their sense, whilst watching the dance. There is no need to act out the words as they happen, but there should be some connection between the words and the dance, at some point and in some way. The choreographer may take images from the words as a starting point for improvisation, or he may adopt the general sense rather than specific passages. Or, like Alston, he may reflect the rhythm of the word patterns.

Sound effect tapes
If you want a background or 'sound environment', consider using a sound effect tape. These include the BBC series of tapes, featuring crowd noises, war, traffic, country sounds, 'death and horror' (with sections entitled 'Dracula's wing beats' or 'women screaming') and many more, all available from Bush House in London and by mail order. Other tapes include 'New Age' ones and those designed for therapeutic relaxation.

Silence
It is possible to work without music at all and dance in silence. This sounds terrifying if you have always choreographed to the music and usually rely on it to 'tell you what to do'!

Every movement has rhythm and dynamics. The heartbeat and pulse, the action of breathing, the cycles of waking and sleeping are all rhythmic activities. Every gesture or natural movement contains a rhythm made up of its preparation, execution and completion. These movements do not need an outside beat, pulse or count to give them rhythmic and dynamic life.

It is sometimes supposed that for movement to become 'dance' it must have musical accompaniment. Also that it must fit with the music's beat. Dance may, indeed, be of the type which 'matches' the music and many dance styles traditionally reflect the musical accompaniment closely.

However, dance is a visual medium. The audience can appreciate movement for its own sake, which exists in its own right and determines its own rhythms. Dance in silence focuses the eye intensely on the dancer's movement, giving a compelling, hypnotic quality. Try to see Richard Alston's solo *Soda Lake* (1981), available commercially on video.

Music and sound resources

Radio and record library The cheapest and easiest way to hear new music is via the radio and local record library. BBC Radio 3 and Classic FM broadcast almost non-stop classical music. The small charge made by record libraries is nothing compared with the cost of buying a tape on the offchance it will be suitable.

Initially, choose tapes containing short pieces: 2 and 3 minute pieces, going up to 4 to 6 minutes, then 6 to 12 minutes. Experience is needed to sustain the choreographic interest in pieces longer than this.

More unusual items can be found in specialist record shops. In London, good general shops are Tower Records, at Piccadilly Circus and Kensington, and Farringdon Records, with a branch in the Festival Hall. The HMV Shop in Oxford Street stocks contemporary music, and for rarities and deletions try Harold Moore's. The Music Discount Centres sell inexpensive tapes; Dance Books stocks tapes and videos as well as books. Enquire about mail order facilities at the above stores. Addresses at the end of the book.

Collaborating with a composer A score specially written for a dance has the advantage of being tailor-made. The chance to create movement and music together, from scratch, is an exciting challenge. In an ideal partnership, each art will contribute to the development of the other, and it can be fun to work in partnership with another artist.

How will you find a composer? Dance musicians and accompanists often compose, or musicians or tutors in a local school, college or music society might be interested. You could certainly write and enquire.

HOW DO COLLABORATIONS WORK? The nature of collaborations varies. A choreographer might use an already written piece and ask the composer for one or two changes; these could include shortening or lengthening the piece, omitting or adding a section, or writing a slightly different ending. Provided that the composer is sympathetic, this should be straightforward. Starting from scratch, it is likely that the choreographer or the composer will take the lead, at least at the beginning. If it is you who is to set the ball rolling, it can be helpful to have a few ideas ready to discuss with the composer and possibly some guidelines.

- The approximate length of the piece is important, even if it is as vague as 'about 5 minutes; or 'between 8 and 10 minutes'.
- Any specifications regarding the type of sound you want: a flute solo, percussion, violin and piano, a brass band, 'house' music, chimes, voice, a blues, etc.
- Any ideas for a dramatic or programmatic theme: dawn, a conflict, gangsters, moonlight on water, a street scene, etc.
- Any idea of mood, mysterious, romantic, harsh, sad, exuberant, etc.

- Details and time-plan of any sections within the total piece: 1 minute cello solo, very sad, followed by the entry of violin and 1–2 minute duet becoming more lively.

For *The Sleeping Beauty*; Petipa's instructions to Tchaikovsky contained dramatic, dance and musical ideas, within a structure defined by his interpretation of the story. These were detailed but allowed Tchaikovsky sufficient freedom to create his magnificent score.

Conversely, in Cunningham and Cage's work, *Fielding Sixes* (1956), the music was randomised and the choreography set. Whilst the dancers performed strictly prescribed movements, five musicians worked with a cassette recorder each, plus a box of 20–30 cassettes of Irish music. They randomly picked a cassette, played it for 30 seconds, then changed its speed for a further 10 seconds. They repeated this process with another tape, throughout the work, which meant that the dancers had to rely mainly on their muscular memory to keep going.

Creating your own score   If you have musical abilities, then you might be able to write your own music. If you can use a synthesiser, it can be fun to create your own sound score. Both these options are rewarding, but can be time-consuming. Do you really have the time to be both the choreographer and composer?

CHOOSING AND USING MUSIC

Apart from the length of a piece, several other factors affect its general suitability:

- It should be a complete piece in its own right. Never cut a composer's work. However a single movement from a longer work may be acceptable. Complete pieces have a structure which give the choreographer a built-in sense of form. The way the musical ideas unfold and develop can assist in the development of the movement.

If you are making a 'sound collage', then occasionally it is justified to cut a composer's work. You should get permission for this, if the composer is still alive, as well as applying for permission to perform the music. (See **copyright** below.) It is also worth asking a musician's opinion when intending to use any 'cut' music for collage purposes.

- Music with a powerful atmosphere will help contribute to the mood of the piece
- Music with rhythmic interest will enhance the choreography
- Music with textural interest will enhance the choreography.

Beware of:

- Music which is too long. Can you sustain the choreographic interest?
- Music which is repetitious, particularly in terms of rhythm. You need to be a skilled choreographer to offset the monotonous effect.
- Music with little dynamic contrast. Again, the choreography will need to be dynamically interesting to keep the audience's attention.
- Music composed on a very large scale, such as symphonies. The length and scope of works like these can tend to overwhelm the movement.

- Music which is very well known, or has been previously choreographed to, particularly if the audience already has its own ideas about what should go with a particular piece of music. I recall Scottish Ballet's performances of *The Nutcracker* in the 1970s where the Mirlitons had to dance to a chorus from the audience of 'Everyone's a fruit and nutcase', Tchaikovsky's music having become popular by its use in an advertisement! Hackneyed music is also a hindrance, unless you are clever enough to pinpoint and focus its very familiarity in the choreography.

Copyright

The use of any music for performance requires the appropriate permissions and licences. Organisations to contact for advice are The Performing Right Society, Phonographic Performance Limited, Mechanical Copyright Protection and The Patent Office. Dance UK also offers an information sheet on the subject to its members, and Ann Whitley's book, *Look before You Leap*, covers copyright and other administrative matters. Addresses at the end of the book.

Basically, permission is needed to perform any work still in copyright. This means that a composer's work is legally protected during his lifetime and for a certain period after his death. Because conditions vary for each individual work, it is necessary to seek the advice of the experts above.

Relating movement to music

This is one of the most fascinating aspects of dance. There are some who believe that the movement must exactly reflect the music or sound from start to finish, and those who consider that the two arts are completely independent.

Within these two extremes lie the most common approaches adopted by choreographers today.

The traditional approach

- The movement generally reflects the music, whether in terms of rhythm, dynamics, texture, speed or volume. Or in the dramatic or programmatic terms of the overall form.
- The movement goes against or through the music. Again, this may be rhythmically, dynamically, texturally or in speed and volume. It is also possible to use the music as a background.
- The movement uses a mixture of the above.

The last can generally be relied upon to give successful results. A good dance piece should complement the music. It should do more than merely mimic the music. The movement should have a rhythmic and dynamic life of its own, and neither lean on the music nor be its slave. This does not mean that the two should bear no relation to each other. On the contrary, the relationship should be multi-faceted.

COMPLEMENTING THE MUSIC To complement rather than just imitate the music's rhythm and dynamics, consider the following:

- even the slowest dance needs moments of faster movement, and an overall fast dance needs slower ones;
- pauses can act as punctuation marks; rather than being 'dead' moments, pauses

can suggest suspension, waiting, repose, collecting one's thoughts, surprise, shock, 'speechlessness' and more;

- with even counts, say in a count of eight, vary the timing of the movements with the pulse; for a symmetrical effect try 4 movements taking 2 counts each, 2 movements taking 4 counts each, or 1 movement taking 8 counts; for an uneven, asymmetrical effect try 2 movements taking 3 and 5 counts each, or 1 and 7 counts each;
- work a movement phrase over and across two musical phrases;
- create a rhythm pattern in movement which complements the musical rhythm pattern;
- use breath, or free rhythm, to the pulse;
- reflect the 'rise-and-fall' in the music;
- allow the music to speak for itself by involving moments of complete stillness, which are longer than pauses;
- keep in mind the fact that all movement contains rhythm and dynamics, as described in the section on use of silence (see page 37).

Non-traditional approaches Some choreographers today are experimenting to discover new ways in which the two arts can work together.

The work of Merce Cunningham with composer John Cage has done much to open up the possibilities of dance and music. The fascination of the rhythm and dynamics inherent in movement, independent of accompaniment, led Cunningham to dispense with the established composer/choreographer relationship, allowing each art to develop its own form, which often come together only at the first performance. Cunningham and Cage also explored the use of chance in choreography and music.

Before you start

Consider the music's rhythm, mood, texture and overall form. Whatever your approach, you must become totally familiar with your chosen music. You must know how it goes from start to finish, its overall form and where the repeats are; its sections, highlights, climaxes and resolutions. Its tunes, rhythms and textures. You must also allow the music to suggest things to you – choreographic ideas such as a particular step, or the feeling that 'this bit sounds like the entry of a lot of people'. Or it could be an emotional undercurrent, the hint of a folk dance, or the suggestion of a place, say a deserted church or urban townscape. Allow it to work on you as much as you work on it!

Choreographers usually devise their own personal notation to identify musical passages. They may count the music, relate to musical landmarks, or use minutes and seconds. It is important to consider how your chosen dancers generally work with music. By this I mean that if they customarily count, it might be difficult for them to get used to taking a visual or aural cue, and you may need to spend some time familiarising them with a new way of working.

Keep an open mind about what you consider would work with a specific dance style. Modern dance works as well with classical music as ballet, and ballet is exciting to an experimental sound score or minimalism.

SOUND IN PERFORMANCE

Live music

Nothing compares with the excitement of live music and the spontaneous interplay between musician and dancer. Financial and scheduling limitations may make it beyond your means, but remember that a solo musician can be as effective as an ensemble, and consider collaborating with a local music group, music college or school.

It is vital that musicians and dancers work together as frequently as possible. It is possible to rehearse to a taped version of the music, preferably one made by the musician(s) who will be playing for the performance, and this may be the most convenient option. But sooner or later, preferably sooner rather than later, the two sets of performers must come together. If the musicians are unused to playing for dance, they and the dancers may be in for a shock. Accompanying dance is a highly specialised task, akin to accompanying singers, but need the additional skill of having to observe the dancer whilst playing. Only through actually watching the dancers will the musicians be able to judge the tempi correctly. If there is a conductor then, of course, he will be in charge of this, but a dance performance often relies on a single musician.

The choreographer should discuss tempi with the conductor or musicians as early as possible in the creative process, preferably as soon as the music is chosen. There exist a wide variety of musical interpretations of a specific piece and the choreographer may have become familiar with a particular one through a commercially available recording. Tempi can affect the length of a piece by several minutes, so it is crucial that your musician knows which version of the music you have been listening to. Choreographers are notorious for gearing their movement round a particular interpretation, only to be devastated when they hear another version. Musicians, too, can have strong ideas about how a piece should be played, whether it is danced to or not. If the musicians are unfamiliar with dance, explain why you want the music a certain way, and above all, show them the choreography with the actual dancers. If your requests are met with resistance, listen to the reasons. There is a difference between sheer stubbornness and the valid reading of a composer's work. The advice of a first-class musician who is sympathetic to the needs of dance is invaluable. Maybe you need to adjust the choreography slightly, maybe the music needs adjusting. Give-and-take is the answer.

Two casts may need different speeds, so ensure that both casts get a proper chance to rehearse. Sometimes the musicians themselves vary from show to show, so organise a rehearsal.

You will need to think whether the music or dancer starts first at the beginning of a section. If they start absolutely together, or the dancer starts first, the exact synchronisation will need practice, and a cueing system will need to be set up. If the dancer and musician can see each other, they can judge it visually, with a mixture of rhythmic sensitivity and ESP, but if they cannot see each other, then the Stage Manager or other person cueing the show will be responsible. If the music is to start on the high point of a *posé* into *arabesque* for example, great precision will be needed by all concerned plus time to practise.

Royal Ballet Education Project: creating the music (PHOTO: © *1996 Angela Taylor*)

Placing of musicians In the theatre, the placing of musicians relative to the dancers is important for visibility and for creating the correct atmosphere. Not all venues have an orchestra pit. Musicians may be part of the stage 'community' like the solo singer of Mahler's *Kindertotenlieder* in Tudor's *Dark Elegies*, seated on a stool at the side of the stage and dressed like the dancers in basic folk costume. In MacMillan's *Elite Syncopations* the ragtime band playing Scott Joplin is seated on a raised platform at the back of the stage. In Robbins' *The Concert* the solo pianist is placed downstage right, whilst the 'concertgoers' of the cast settle themselves on collapsible seats facing across the stage towards the piano.

In Christopher Bruce's *Waiting* (1993), with music by Errolyn Wallen, the dancers became musicians by beating out rhythms on the metallic surfaces which formed the set – corrugated iron walls, roofs and railings acting as percussion instruments on which the dancers stamped and battered out their frustration. In Fergus Early's works for Green Candle, the dancers and musicians interchange and intermix freely, dancers playing instruments and singing, and musicians moving.

In the absence of a pit or the musicians being 'part of the action', their placing needs thought. Possibilities are between audience and dancers to one side of the stage, provided that the dancing area can still be seen by conductor or musicians, and they do not obstruct the audience's view. Players, instruments, chairs and music stands take up space; electronic equipment needs cabling and a convenient power source; there may also be microphones and lights. These requirements should be considered at the outset. The poor musician is sometimes seated in the wings, out of sight of the audience. Unless there is an artistic reason for this, like the sound 'coming from an invisible source', there seems no point in hiding your live music!

A piano needs to be placed exactly where it is needed and checked that it is in tune. Annie Lincoln, Stage Manager of English National Ballet, says that on small-scale tours, where a piano reduction of the score is used instead of the orchestra, one of the first considerations in a venue is getting the piano positioned in the right spot. If it needs moving far, or to or from another level, whoever is doing the heavy work needs adequate warning. She comments that occasionally the buck is passed concerning this responsibility and she is told 'the piano can't be moved'. All her Stage Manager's traditional diplomacy, authority and powers of persuasion may be needed to communicate that 'no piano' means 'no show'.

Recorded music and sound

If prerecorded, a high quality of sound should be ensured, to which contribute:

- the clarity of the original recording
- the quality of the mastertape
- the calibre of the equipment on which it is to be played.

Work backwards from the sound equipment, if any, in the venue, as this can range from the proverbial sublime to the ridiculous. A well-equipped theatre should present no problems, but if the performance is in a gymnasium or church hall, there may be no equipment whatsoever, so, if you do not possess adequate portable equipment, you will need to hire or borrow.

The equipment available will dictate the format of your mastertape, which contains all prerecorded music and sound on a single tape. It may be made as:

REEL TO REEL TAPE This is commonly used, generally gives good sound reproduction, and is easy to cue in performance. There are different speeds. Check out the speed before you make the mastertape.

CASSETTE All sound desks have cassette decks which are simple to use. Precise cueing may not be as easy as the reel-to-reel. Cassettes can sometimes contain hiss from the duplicating process, and this can obscure the clarity of sound. However, a good-quality cassette recording is a reliable option if facilities are basic. A cassette back-up tape is always essential in case something goes wrong with your main source.

CD AND MINI DISC A sound technician may be able to record your pieces onto a CD, which has excellent sound quality. A mini disc, which is another form of recordable CD, is a more recent and less common alternative, requiring special reproduction equipment.

DAT TAPE DAT stands for Digital Audio Tape. It is a recording medium which utilises digital technology, giving very high-quality sound reproduction. It is virtually hiss-free and is easy to cue. This is another comparatively recent introduction, popular with musicians but requiring special reproduction equipment.

It is important that the sound reproduction in the venue is capable of providing sufficient amplification for the size of the auditorium. It should also be of a high enough standard to ensure the clarity of the musical sound. Ideally you should experiment beforehand with the equipment in situ, and if you are bringing in equip-

*Reel-to-reel sound
equipment*
(PHOTO: *author*)

ment to a space such as a gymnasium, try out whatever you can get hold of in advance. Stand in all parts of the audience area and listen to the sound. A portable CD and cassette deck used in such a hall may be woefully inadequate in providing adequate volume. Several factors contribute to this: the sheer size of the space, the height of the ceiling and the distance between audience and speakers. The number of people present in a hall can also make a difference, as they tend to soak up the sound, so the volume in an empty space will sound greater than when there is a large audience.

Ideally, you will have a sound technician to oversee these aspects, and he may double up as musician, stage manager or lighting technician. However, it is always useful to have some knowledge of the subject yourself.

Sound technology has made rapid developments in recent years, and the wide availability of high-quality recordings on cassette and CD has raised expectations of sound quality in a live performance. A dance performance should not require a complicated sound set-up, but certain basic needs must be met, requiring specific equipment, as follows:

- tape deck on which the recording is played
- amplifiers to control the amount of sound emitted
- loudspeakers, positioned where both audience and performers can hear the sound; the audibility needed for the performers onstage, known as foldback, is important for dance, where the relationship of music and movement is paramount
- optional mixing desk.

When checking equipment on site, you may find some facilities available which are unsuitable, such as the PA systems in halls not primarily used for dance performances. 'PA' stands for 'public address', and this is precisely what they are intended for, and their quality of sound reproduction is often too rough to do justice to a musical score. In this case, it would be better to take your own sound equipment, hired if necessary. This will need setting up, and the whole process of choosing, hiring and installing equipment is best undertaken by a sound technician.

The sound *operator* should also be considered, and must be able actually to operate the equipment. A whizz-kid with a ghetto-blaster in a studio may be quite clueless when confronted by a DAT machine, reel-to-reel or mini disc. Skills include cueing starts and stops, adjusting volume and tone, and ideally being able to troubleshoot if something breaks down. Faults occur in various parts of the system and, if they happen mid-show, are a nightmare. Common problems include a loose wire (in the tape deck, amplifier or speakers) or a blown fuse, resulting in a complete loss of sound. For such eventualities you should always have a back-up, whether a ghetto-blaster plus cassette or CD or, with more sophisticated equipment, a cassette deck back-up to a reel-to-reel or a DAT machine. The important thing is for the performance to continue, whilst the fault is being rectified. If the sound is not completely lost, wait for a break in the show to solve the problem. One of the speakers may have broken, leaving only partial sound, or a reel-to-reel tape may have been wound on incorrectly, wrong side uppermost, resulting in muzzy reproduction.

The DAT tape, popular with musicians for its excellent reproduction, is used increasingly for performances, but due to its digital recording, can be alarming if it goes wrong. I have known the sound on a DAT tape jump around for several seconds, then right itself without interference and give perfect sound! For this reason only, I hesitate to recommend the exclusive use of DAT tapes, although they give marvellous clarity of sound and are easy and silent to cue.

Whatever your equipment, the quality of the original recording is crucial. CDs generally give the best sound, and cassette tapes and records should ideally be new and unused. This is to eliminate crackles, hiss and other distortions which arise from wear and tear. A little hiss can be removed by mixing when the mastertape is made, but good equipment reproduces with great clarity and does not distinguish between music, scratches and crackles.

The mastertape It is general practice to make a mastertape of the whole performance, with all prerecorded music and sound put onto one tape, to eradicate the messy and time-consuming business of inserting a different tape into the machine for each item. It also allows the technician to assess the overall sound quality. If the show contains a number of short pieces, he may be presented with a variety of sound sources and musical styles. It is not uncommon to have a classical guitar piece on CD, followed by a 'technofunk' number on cassette, followed by a choral work on record. The recordist's job is to ensure the mastertape reproduces all pieces equally well, and sound technicians have a range of possibilities at their fingertips with ever-increasing technological facilities for mixing. They do a highly-skilled job, and you should find the best person you can afford to make your mastertape. As well as the DAT, CD or reel-to-reel tape you need for the venue, you will need at least one back-up cassette, plus copies for use in the studio. DAT tapes are tiny and insignificant-looking, so be careful not to lose the crucial mastertape!

Cueing the sound The sound operator should be able to see the performance area clearly, with equipment set up in place which ensures this. In a theatre, there should be no problem but, in a less formal situation, with perhaps a limited number of electrical outputs, it may be necessary for the sound desk to be in the auditorium or at one side of the performance area. Even if cues are given by the Stage Manager, it is still helpful for the operator to have a clear view of the action; if the operator is taking the cues directly, it is essential.

Sound and lighting cues in a theatre are given by the Stage Manager, through microphones or 'cans', to the technicians in the backstage or auditorium area. The Stage Manager must be totally familiar with the cues, and have sufficient practice at delivery. In a show with many short items and a variety of cueing techniques, the observation needed can be formidable. A dance may start in silence, with a visual cue for the sound taken from a specific movement by the dancers. A technician unfamiliar with dance may be baffled when told to start the sound on the leading dancer's third arabesque across the stage, or when the last dancer in a contemporary dance does her second contraction. The latter may sound as if one of the cast is about to give birth. Experience of dance and familiarity with the specific piece is necessary if the cueing is to be effective.

5. Design _____

Some choreographers today have rejected the notion of theatrical design altogether, whilst others work closely with designers where set installations and costumes may actively initiate choreographic ideas.

So the approach will depend on the style and working methods of choreographer and designer, and the resources available: costume maker, set builder, funds, time, space and technical facilities.

The ideal situation is to collaborate with a designer experienced in dance, so establish at the outset whether your designer has worked with dance before. Dancers have to be able to move in their costumes and it is vital that this is understood before the making up begins. Dance design is not yet an established part of all theatre design courses, so many designers learn 'on the job'. An experienced designer should be able to take your ideas, watch the movement and come up with suggestions which will work within your budget. These may match what you have in mind; ideally, they will surpass it!

If you cannot afford a designer, then it will be up to you. Designs traditionally comprise set and costumes. However, if you cannot afford a designer, it is unlikely you can afford a set builder, so you may decide to have costumes only. Sets will be abandoned until you are in a position to afford them. The absence of a set is not a disaster and at least you know the entire space will be free for the dancers.

GENERAL PRINCIPLES

- The designs must enhance and support the concept of the dance.
- There should be a unity between costumes and scenic elements.
- The costume designs must work with the movements.
- The costume designs should flatter the dancers.
- The designs must be able to be constructed within the limitations of money, time and expertise.

The designs must enhance and support the concept of the dance
The choreographer and designer must talk in depth at the outset, discussing theme, music or sound, and the number, type and gender of dancers (plus ages if children are involved). Also any influences such as a particular period, national characteristic or other art form (such as a painting, sculpture or poem). The choreographer should indicate movement characteristics to be taken into account, such as high leg extensions (which would require that the costumes allow sufficient freedom of movement), *pointe* work, tap or Spanish dance (which require special footwear), or somersaults (which affect headwear and hairdos).

At this stage, the choreographer should offer any basic suggestions like 'a heavy skirt'. or 'waistcoats', 'a cloak' or 'coloured gloves', and hints regarding atmosphere ('dark and brooding', 'frothy and effervescent', 'it's really a big send-up', or 'sultry and glamorous'). Also hints about personality 'like Carmen Miranda', 'like Madonna', 'like Michael Jackson' or 'Pride and Prejudice', 'The Muppets', etc.).

Sometimes he visualises the type of lighting and can tell the designer, 'It takes place in moonlight', or 'There will be flashing disco lights', or 'I hope this will be a leafy gobo'.

The designs should also be an integral and balanced part of the total concept. They should not dominate or overwhelm the movement and dancers in terms of colour, pattern or mass. Some costumes look as if 'they are wearing the dancer' rather than the other way round, and a backcloth can occasionally be so eye-catching that it is a distraction from the movement. A set that is too busy can obscure the dancers' lines.

The designer's job is to enhance the mood, period and any ethnic flavour. He must also decide whether a 'literal' or more 'abstract' treatment is appropriate. Say a dance contained elements of an Elizabethan court dance. This could be an attempt to reproduce a dance as authentically as possible, demanding an 'authentic' costume. Alternatively, the dance might be a modern one, with just a flavour of the period. The two design treatments in this case would be very different: the former requiring a heavy skirt, voluminous underwear and a traditional Elizabethan collar. The latter might be based on an all-in-one, decorated with period designs and patterns.

There should be a unity between costumes and scenic elements
Good design will have a unified look. There will be a connection between all the elements. Sets and costumes will work together.

The costume designs must work with the movements
The costumes must allow the movements to happen, be comfortable and not cause the dancers to worry about ripping an armhole or losing a shoe. If substantial partner-work is involved, including lifts, or even throws, the lifted dancer should not have bulky fabric round the waist, preventing her partner from getting a grip. Nor should there be any fiddly decoration in which his fingers could get caught.

If the dancers spend time very close together, or touching, then anything sticking out beyond the contour of the body will get in the way. This applies to large wigs and headdresses as well as other protuberances.

If there is 'upside down' work, a skirt must have appropriate underwear. You should also check if the skirt conceals the dancer's body, arms and head for the period they are upside down. This can look comical, which is fine if comedy is intended!

There are also artistic considerations which are unique to dance. If the movements contain very fluid lines, then 'solid' or 'square' designs can dilute the effect. A designer may wish deliberately to contrast flowing lines with a 'hard' environment in the set, but sometimes the two conflict by accident and to no effect. A serious treatment of a theme, choreographically, could be nullified if the designs tended towards the comical. So the choreographer and designer must decide whether the two should be 'in harmony' or whether a deliberate contrast is appropriate.

Unity not uniformity (PHOTOS: *Tony King*)

The costume designs should flatter the dancers

Whilst there may be occasions where the dancers are intended to look strange, ugly or distorted, they should never look like this through bad design or clumsy construction.

This demands that the designer is realistic about the specific bodies of the dancers. There is no point in creating a design around a 6ft hunk, if the reality is to be danced by a 5ft 3in stripling. A shiny white all-in-one will not suit a 4ft 11in fourteen-year-old with puppy fat.

Vertical lines lengthen and fine down a body, whereas horizontal lines shorten and widen. The horizontal and shortening effect made by 'cutting a body in half' at the waist must also be borne in mind.

Dark colours are generally slimming and pale ones tend to enlarge the shape. Bulky fabric always makes a dancer look larger. People consider that a plump dancer will look better with a lot of loose draping fabric round the waist. This is a fallacy. The fabric will add even more inches.

Unity versus uniformity

Costumes need not be identical. Identical costumes look like a uniform. This may be appropriate, but it can occur by accident.

Unity, without uniformity, can be given to a set of costumes if they have certain things in common, whilst still retaining an individuality. This could be done very simply by putting the whole cast in, say, black leggings. Each dancer could have a completely individual top but the leggings would link them all together.

Or the unity could be in terms of colour. The whole cast could be in blue, but all different shades.

Or the unity could be in overall shape: everyone could be in fitted trousers with an overshirt.

The advantage of unity over uniformity is that it allows each dancer individuality. Also, uniformity makes a strong statement in itself. When do people dress identically? Uniforms have strong associations for most people, suggesting school, the forces, police, hospital, priston, etc.

The designs can be constructed within the limitations of money, time and expertise

The section on fabrics discusses where they may be bought cheaply. The amount of fabric needed for an effect or costume is crucial. Do not consider full silk cloaks for a cast of twenty, or even ten, unless you have lots of money. Even a circular skirt, which on average need 4 metres of 115 cm (45in.) fabric if it is to hang and move well, is expensive when multiplied by a cast of eight. A 'sea' or 'river' effect, which can be achieved by rippling a large quantity of silk over the floor, costs a bomb! Dance shoes are expensive, so do not expect your dancers to have many sets of *pointe* shoes for dyeing, unless you are paying the bill (they cost about £30 a pair).

Your costume maker's expertise will also determine how ambitious you can be. If you do not have basic tailoring skills, a fitted bodice will be difficult to make, and you should consider using a leotard as a base, and disguising it to look like a bodice. For tutus, go to a specialist or contact your nearest ballet company or vocational school, and ask to hire or borrow.

6. Sets

The history of dance design has shown various trends in sets – from painted backcloths and flats, to stage 'constructions' and sculpture, to a bare dancing area, devoid of sets altogether. With the increasing contribution made by lighting, some groups nowadays rely on minimal sets, meaning less expense and easier touring.

Broadly speaking, sets for dance consist of free-standing or hung items. Dance groups with minimal resources should consider any scenic items carefully. The advantage of a set is that it can transform the performing space. However, there are a number of problems with both free-standing and hung sets, which can be difficult to solve without technical expertise and facilities.

The expense of sets has already been mentioned. You may have a father, husband or boyfriend, into DIY, who will build some flats for you. These take a lot of materials, which must pass fire regulations, and need to be totally stable, as well as easy to set up in the performing space. Avoid sets unless you are completely confident in your designer, maker, finances, transport and stage crew.

Even some professional groups are cautious with sets, and the good thing about dance is that the movement often makes them unnecessary.

Backcloth and masking

All theatres will have a backcloth and masking. Masking is the means whereby the sidelights and wings are concealed or 'masked' from the audience's view. This is usually achieved by a series of cloths, or 'legs' hanging at the side at varying distances from the front of the stage to the back. Each theatre will have its own number of legs, relative to the depth of the stage.

You may be asked what sort of backcloth and masking you want. In this case, ask what the possibilities are. Usually, they are 'a black box' or 'a white box'. These mean a black backcloth and black masking, or a white cyclorama (cyc). Or a grey backcloth and grey legs. which can look drab if not well lit. A white cyc allows colour to be thrown onto it by the lights and can give a clean, spacious look. A black surround will not allow light to be projected onto it, but it looks neat and clean, and the dancers, particularly if they are in pale or bright colours, will stand out clearly.

Spaces with no backcloth and masking

Gymnasiums and other 'open' spaces will have no backcloth and masking, so you will need to take in and erect your own, or dance without them. If the former, you will have the challenge of tying up the curtains on a girder, or pole, which is time consuming.

Folding screens can be used as 'legs' at the sides, to make wings.

However, the movement is the thing, and an open, bare, arena-like space can work very well. Better, in fact, than a cluttered space. So don't worry if you have no backcloth or masking. Just ensure the dancers rehearse their entrances and exits,

Students hanging curtains
(PHOTO: *author*)

which will be in full view of the audience, and stand still when they are waiting to come on. Children and students tend to fidget. When there are no wings, the following are taboo:

- pulling the leotard down over the backside; this is a dancer's favourite pastime after making an exit – second only in popularity to
- adjusting the hairdo – followed by
- scratching the nose
- standing with hands on hips or arms folded
- chattering.

It is also important that the dancers do not knock, brush, or push legs or backcloth as they make entrances and exits. As well as being distracting, this is dangerous, as the structures may topple over.

Practising entrances and exits ensures that the dancers continue 'in character' until they are completely out of sight of the audience or, if remaining in view, choose the correct moment to finish walking, running or whatever else their exit involves, and unobtrusively come to a stop.

A waiting dancer must not distract from the action onstage – particularly true when there is no masking.

A final thought for spaces without backcloth and legs is that a portable dance floor can enhance the look, delineate the dance area and create a 'magic space'.

Hung items

Cloths, gauzes and screens will have to be hung on a lighting bar, and 'flown' in and out, requiring a venue with flying facilities. Only a well-equipped theatre will have flying facilities. School halls, gymnasiums, community centres and similar sites are unlikely to have them.

It is sometimes possible to attach a cloth to a girder in the ceiling of a non-theatre space. This means someone going up a ladder and tying a large cloth onto the girder. This takes considerable time. Once it is up, it will need to be pulled straight. If it is meant to be flat, then any folds must be smoothed out; if it is meant to have folds, these must hang straight down. The cloth will also need to be rolled neatly at the bottom, and weighted, so that it does not move or blow around in the breeze, and so that any spare material is not tripped on.

In addition, the cloth must be long enough to reach from the height of the girder, right down to the floor. If it is to act as a backcloth, then it must also be wide enough to cover most of its width. It is exactly like finding curtains for a window; you have to get the measurements of width and drop absolutely correct.

Now you are getting an idea of just how large this cloth will need to be, how versatile it will need to be to hang in more than one venue (with different height and width), and how many people it will take to lift, as well as to hang it. How will you get such a large item to and from your venue? Do you have a big enough van?

I am presenting the practical issues rather than the artistic ones first, because unless you can solve the practical problems, you will be wasting your time considering the artistic side. An ill-fitting, badly hung cloth, out of proportion to the whole dance space will scream 'amateur' and 'pretentious', and will detract from good choreography and dancing.

If you are absolutely confident that you can deal with the technical and transport aspects, then consider what effect you want your hung items to make. This is the job of the designer, and should be planned in conjunction with the costumes and lighting.

Cloths may be hung in any part of the stage depth, not just at the back, and may also be in the form of narrow strips, rather like those of a large vertical blind. They may be made of sheer or opaque materials, be plain or decorated, and hung taut or billowing. You will need to find someone to construct the cloth according to the designer's instructions, and you will obviously have to pay for the materials. You could contact your local theatre, and enquire who makes their sets.

If your venue has a white cyclorama, you could try projecting a design onto it. If the venue has a projector, you may need only to produce a slide. This could prove simpler than making a cloth.

Free-standing sets

Whilst free-standing sets do not have the problems associated with hung items, they still need transporting and setting up. Even a well-established, professional company like Green Candle has sets specially constructed so that they can be packed easily in their van. Green Candle's sets are made in several sections, so that they can be made larger or smaller, to adapt to the different size spaces the company dances in. They must also be small enough to get in through the door or loading bay!

The size of the dancing space is crucial when considering free-standing items; it must be sufficiently large to accommodate the set and the dancers. A set which crowds the dancers, or appears so tiny as to be irrelevant, will appear amateurish.

A set must contribute so that the dance would not work without it. It must be an integral part of the action. It may be realistic and represent a house, or a symbolic or abstract feature. The exact placing of free-standing items is important. Dancers may be moving round or behind them, and need enough room to execute the choreography without knocking them, or looking cramped.

If you have a friend good at carpentry who offers to make a free-standing set for you, talk to the designer and discover the exact size the set needs to be, relative to the dimensions of the dancing space, including the height of the ceiling. He must ensure that the set is made in non-inflammable materials; otherwise it may be banned under the venue's fire regulations. A serious amateur should refer to a book like *Create Your Own Stage Sets* by Terry Thomas.

If a set would not be appropriate in your circumstances, don't despair. Consider the masterpieces by Balanchine, where he deliberately stripped the stage bare of scenic elements. This was not because he did not have the resources for a set and, indeed, he did create notable ballets with designers like Eugene Berman. However, he felt that the dance could and should stand on its own. After all, his ballets used line and shape to such a sophisticated and complex degree in the movement that sets became redundant. So you can concentrate on making the dance itself so interesting that the audience does not notice whether there is a set or not!

However, it is still good to dream of the time when you will have the opportunity to work with a designer on a set for your work. The Jiving Lindy Hoppers, another well-established, professional company, comment that the first time they had the luxury of working with a designer was after they had become successful, not before!

Here are examples of what has been done with sets for dance, when funding and resources allow. Let them inspire you for the future.

Construction-based sets

Constructions make interesting and effective sets, and include those which actually involve the choreography and dancers, as well as those acting as a background or surround.

One of the most famous constructions is Rouben Ter-Arutinian's white scaffolding for Tetley's *Pierrot Lunaire* (1962), inspired by the choreographer's memory of the jungle gym of his childhood. The scaffolding represents many things to Pierrot; as Glen Tetley says in interview (*Dance Month*, BBC TV. 1979), 'It is his tower, his bed, the springboard for his love affair with the moon ... at the beginning Pierrot is high, drunk on the moonlight and his dreams of youth.' Choreographically, as well as metaphorically, he is indeed high, swinging, suspended at the very top of the scaffolding.

Throughout the piece, the construction is exploited symbolically and practically, with many actions and dramatic moments involving the dancers moving on, in and through the structure. Without the scaffolding, much of the choreography would cease to exist, and this factor provides a yardstick by which the necessity for, and success of, such a set may be judged.

Rehearsing on a construction-based set, students from Elmhurst Ballet School try out Andy Radford's set for Lynn Seymour's The Dorm. *(PHOTO: Focus on Dance)*

Water as a scenic element

Companies with sufficient funds and facilities have also introduced other innovative means of set design. Siobhan Davies and designer David Buckland used water in *Make Make* (1992), where it streamed like rain down a vast window-like structure at the back of the stage. Water was also used in Lloyd Newson's *Strange Fish* (1992) for DV8 Physical Theatre, where designer Peter J. Davison's stage floor opened to reveal a deep expanse of water underneath.

Other staging

The choreographers Davies and Newson are at the forefront of adventurous staging, their collaborations involving sets, costume and lighting as equal partners with the movement. Newson's masterwork, *Enter Achilles* (1995) for DV8 Physical Theatre, with a superlative city bar set by Ian MacNeil, exploited different levels, with a 20ft-high platform and a rope, high up on which an aerial encounter took place, and a stage floor which, in a striking *coup de théâtre*, shook and wrenched itself to vertical, erupting from underneath and destroying the bar. Newson confirms that the company has fought long and hard to be in the position where it has funds and time to produce work of this calibre and technical adventurousness, and new pieces are created only after much research and an extensive rehearsal period.

Some companies specialise in productions featuring fantastic costume, scenic and lighting effects, often concealing or distoring the human body: American Alwin Nikolais in particular, pioneered a unique style of movement theatre and spectacle in this vein, whose offshoots include the companies Pilobolus and Momix.

SAFETY

With complex stagings like these, it is absolutely essential that all scenic elements, constructions, and costumes be fully worked in, for reasons of safety as well as artistry. Even simple items, such as rostra, stage ramps and steps must be tested for security by the dancers, especially if dance movements are to be performed on them.

During the creation of Ballet Rambert's children show, 'Bertram Batell's Sideshow', in the 1970s, I appeared as a fly in Peter Curtis's ballet *Cobweb*. Needless to say, a giant cobweb was the chief scenic element, and a huge army scrambling net was affixed to the beams of the rehearsal room to enable the choreography to be worked out on the net. Part of my role included a dance of struggle high up on the cobweb, and on the day when Marie Rambert came to watch the rehearsal in progress, I put so much passion into it that the whole net fell down from the ceiling, complete with the spider and myself!

So, take heed that dancers must work in and test scenic elements. Even if they are perfectly safe, the dancers must always treat them carefully, and must concentrate fully when they are dancing in, on, or through them.

Site-specific work
In site-specific works, the choreography and staging are created around a particular place or environment. This may be indoors or out, and the 'site' may be synonymous with the venue, often with extraordinary results. Lea Anderson's production, *Car*, for The Cholmondeleys took place in and around a car. Was the car the site, the set or the venue? The distinctions become blurred in events like this!

Screens and projections
Screens and projections can be used to give many different effects. Screens need to be hung or flown. It is also possible to project onto a screen which is free-standing. This could be a non-theatrical screen which is intended for everyday use with a projector. You would need to assess the size of the screen, relative to whole dance space, to ensure it neither dwarfs the dancers nor is too small to make much impact. The success of projections used for dance depends largely on what is projected and its relevance to the movement taking place. The advantages of using projections are:

- you can change them during the dance
- they can create a series of different environments
- they can can help to change mood and atmosphere
- they can sometimes 'make a point' relative to the movement
- they can represent something, such as a train timetable, a painting or graffiti.

Artist Richard Smith created a mobile set containing huge, brightly coloured kite-like screens for Richard Alston's *Wildlife* (1984) for Rambert. These were hung at varying heights, and turned and moved in and out, up and down almost as part of the choreography, and acted as an exotic habitat for the dancers/wildlife contained therein.

Stage levels
Drama productions traditionally use rostra for different levels in a set design, as they do not normally need the large areas of flat stage essential for dance. However,

designers and choreographers have collaborated to incorporate stage levels in notably imaginative ways for many dance works.

Stage levels have tended to be used as part of realistic sets, with steps and staircases requiring the dancers to perform naturalistic movements such as walking or running on them – albeit for highly theatrical and dramatic effects – rather than multiple *pirouettes* and *entrechat* sixes. In MacMillan's *Romeo and Juliet* (1965) Juliet's run down Nicholas Georgiadis' curved staircase from her balcony, to meet Romeo for the Balcony Scene *pas de deux*, is a stunning and moving moment of theatre. Aurora's entrance in Act 1 of *The Sleeping Beauty* traditionally involves stepping down onto the stage for the Rose Adagio, the doll Coppélia always appears seated on a balcony in the ballet of the same name and Ashton makes great comic play on Osbert Lancaster's staircase up to Lise's bedroom in Act 2 of *La Fille Mal Gardée*.

Alternatively, levels can be achieved by the use of constructions such as the scaffolding tower of *Pierrot Lunaire*, already mentioned.

Height can be exploited by the use of aerial work, traditionally a circus skill, but increasingly being incorporated into dance, notably in Newson's *Enter Achilles*, where two men engage in an eloquent duet suspended on a rope high above the stage.

Suspension on part of the sculptural set constituted the final dramatic image of Norman Morrice's *Hazard* (1967) for Rambert, with the leading make dancer hanging high up from a bull's horn-like construction by Nadine Baylis.

These examples are part of the movement conception and they demand the choreographic use of their possibilities. Levels are also about depth below, or its simulation, the latter being exploited in Ian Murray-Clark's swimming pool set for Robert Cohan's humorous *Waterless Method of Swimming Instruction* (1974). Here the bottom of the pool was the stage floor, with the pool's sides and surrounding area created by a naturalistic set, built up on three sides, with the audience seated as if in a submerged viewing chamber on the fourth side. Female dancers 'dived' and somersaulted from the 'poolside' into the arms of the males 'already in the water'.

7. Props_____

Props need careful consideration; if they are not used well, they can be distracting. The main consideration is that they should be fully integrated with the movement and be an essential part of it. It is no good coming on holding something merely as an appendage, and which serves no useful purpose. One traditional useful purpose has been to incorporate a prop into a dance for a young child; a basket, ball, teddy or umbrella has saved many a canny teacher from having to worry about the child's hand and arm movements!

Noguchi created large symbolic structures for Graham which were both prop and costume: in *Errand into the Maze* (1947), the male figure, representing heroine Ariadne's fear, is presented as a menacing, horned, bull-like character who has a huge wooden yoke on his back. He is permanently attached to this encumbrance, and it gives rise to weighty, tortured movements. In *Cave of the Heart* (1946), Medea is shown taking a spiky metallic construction from the set, and donning it like a cloak; it is the crown of serpents and she moves about the stage within its mass of sharp spines. A good choreographer will incorporate a prop imaginatively – the Garland Dance in *The Sleeping Beauty* uses the semi-circular garland base as part of the arm lines and spatial patterns. Ashton's use of satin ribbons in *La Fille Mal Gardée* (1960), particularly in the opening *pas de deux* of Lise and Colas, and later in the Elssler *pas de deux*, which also involves the *corps* of Lise's friends, is exemplary. Christopher Bruce's exploitation of the dramatic and choreographic possibilities of a single wooden chair, in *Swansong*, is masterly.

Primary considerations with a prop are:

- what purpose does it serve?
- is it essential to the dance?
- will it give rise to choreographic ideas, or will it hinder them?
- is it historically or ethnically necessary, and if so, is your use of it authentic?
- does it help to tell the story?
- is it used as a symbol?
- will you make it, or will you 'find' it in a shop?
- is it easily transportable?
- will it pass the fire regulations in the venue?

What you are going to do with the prop when you are not using it. Are you going to put it down? If so, where? On the floor? This sounds obvious, but I have seen choreographers start a dance with a cane, a cloak, a cigarette holder or a bag and happily create for two minutes, then run out of ideas and look for somewhere to get rid of the prop!

Before committing yourself to a prop, find out what you can really do with it. It is important to practise with it, rather than just imagine it. The *actual* object is different from an imaginary one. Its weight, texture and size will all affect how it is used.

Props which do things, like umbrellas which can be opened and shut, need to be tried out for timing. How long does it really take to put the brolly up? Ten counts or ten seconds?

Some simple props

Simple props which do not need to be specially made, include the following:

Scarves Very long silk scarves can suggest waves, clouds, wings, mist, wind and so on. I have choreographed around 2 metre lengths of 90 cm (35in.) wide light silk habotai (from Whaley's by mail order). These can be dyed in seconds, and you can make stunning effects with different colours and patterns, very simply. Pure silk allows the scarf to float, rather than flap. It should be used in such a way that the air is caught in the silk, like a parachute. Synthetic material does not have the same effect as silk; it doesn't catch the air and simply goes flat. These scarves can be used in the air or arranged on the floor to make a 'sea' or 'river'. Simple running, with the dancer holding the scarf high overhead, so that it streams out behind her, can look wonderful.

Fans These may be the Spanish or the Japanese type, which are used differently. Try out many different ways of using the fans; experiment with wrist, hand and arm movements, with the position of the fans, with opening and closing them, and concealing the face. Fan quickly and slowly, and try a fan in each hand. Fan seductively, angrily, wearily, nervously, crazily, drunkenly.

A chair An imaginative choreographer can do many things with a chair. The most obvious involve sitting and standing; try placing the chair facing different ways and sit in different positions (on, under, behind, in front, sideways on, beside, close to, separate from it). Wrap yourself round it, make it a prison, a place of safety, a support, a tree, a car, a bed, a weapon, a look-out tower, a cave. Turn it upside down, pick it up, throw it (carefully!), flee from it, caress it, thump it, hide behind it, snuggle up to it, wear it, eat it.

Different types of chair give different effects. Consider the above with a folding chair, an armchair, a swivel chair, a chair with arms, a chair without arms, a director's chair, a deckchair, a throne, a wheelchair.

A stool As for the chair, consider the effects of a bar stool, a 'milking' stool, a piano stool, a meditation stool.

A hat stand A hat stand can be a useful prop, particularly if you need somewhere to hang bits of costume. It can also suggest place, such as a cloakroom, an entrance hall, a dressing room, a boutique.

A screen A screen can suggest place, you can drape bits of lightweight costume on it, and you can also go behind it. American comedienne Carol Channing did a whole one-woman show using only a single folding screen onstage as a prop. She used this to change behind, whilst carrying on with her act. Simple and elegant.

Use of prop: Koen Onzia, Matz Skoog and Kevin Richmond in Christopher Bruce's Swansong *for English National Ballet* (PHOTO: *Angela Taylor*)

USING PROPS INSTEAD OF A SET

A group of props can replace a set. They can suggest time and place, and are easier to transport. You can use them as Peter Darrell did in *Picnic* (1978). He set the piece in the Edwardian period, with a group of young people going on a picnic. They brought on a picnic basket and laid a white tablecloth out on the floor, on which they set out plates, cups, cutlery and napkins. This constituted a simple setting, which remained onstage throughout the piece and provided a focal point.

Another set of props might be a table and chairs, or stools. Depending on the style of table and chairs, place and time could be suggested, without the use of a set. You could suggest a café, a garden, a kitchen, a canteen, a classroom, a waiting room, a conference room, a card game.

Masks
Masks make wonderfully theatrical props and costumes. For dance, though, they need careful thought. The first concern is that the dancer can perform all the complex movements required whilst wearing the mask; she needs to be able to see all round

her, and this includes the floor. There is a big difference between acting in a mask, and dancing in one. Depending on their size, weight, shape and construction, masks can be very awkward to dance in, and possibly even dangerous. They must not hinder the use of the head, and *pirouettes* and other turns are impossible in a very heavy mask. Partner work, with one or both dancers in a mask, can be tricky.

This said, however, if you get a good mask-maker, and allow plenty of time (not the night before, or even the week before the show – you need much longer) for the dancers to work in them and adjust them if necessary, masks can be dramatic and exciting. Consider full-face or half masks, soft fabric masks or those in hard materials, ethnic masks, *Commedia del Arte* masks, animal masks, neutral masks, hand-held masks. There are many possibilities.

8. Costumes and Make-up

> Why silk? Because it moves. It's natural, made by worms. Nylon doesn't move, it's made by machines.
>
> George Balanchine in *Costumes by Karinska*, by Toni Bentley

Dance costumes take many forms: dazzling, sequinned ballroom dresses, the stylised tutu, classical and Romantic, national dress like the Scottish kilt, Indian sari, Japanese kimono, and the ubiquitous uniform of stretchy bodystocking.

SHOES AND FOOTWEAR

Dance footwear is a specialised area. The makers of dance shoes occupy a privileged position in the hierarchy of theatre costume, and deservedly so, when you consider the particulars of making, for example, a *pointe* shoe. The average dancegoer may not appreciate the finer points of a well-made *pointe* shoe: the varying stiffnesses of the back, the shape of the block and vamp, the mystery of the platform! Do they realise that dancers 'refurbish' ageing *pointes* by hardening them with shellac or custom-made *pointe* shoe hardener or paint over them with shoe paint?

Apart from the aesthetics of the look, and the comfort of the dancer, the question of safety and avoidance of injury is paramount in all dance shoes.

Whilst flat shoes do not require such detailed attention as *pointes*, they do exist in various styles for both men and women. They are made in leather, canvas and satin, with a choice of soles, either leather or suede and consisting of a 'whole' sole, or the recently popular 'split sole'. Leather tends to be good for durability, but canvas clings to the foot more closely, giving a cleaner line, so may be preferred for performance. Shoes should blend in with the leg line for elegance and length; matt tights blend with matt shoes and ribbons, hence the popularity of nylon ribbons and the painting down of shiny satin *pointe* shoes. Balanchine, however, preferred shiny satin ribbons and *pointe* shoes, wishing to draw the attention to the foot. With flat shoes you can match canvas shoes with matt tights and leather or satin shoes with shiny lycra.

THE WARDROBE TEAM

One or several, skilled costume makers, who will work for payment within your means, are worth their weight in gold. Ideally they will come by personal recommendation but, if not, you must establish how familiar they are with dance costumes as distinct from those for drama, opera, pantomime or everyday clothing.

Therefore it may be best to ask at local dance institutions, groups and schools for advice, and if you see costumes in a performance that catch your eye, then try to contact the people involved. Even if they cannot help, they will be flattered to be asked and may suggest another good designer or costume maker.

Once contact has been made, the choreographer, designer and costume maker should get to know each other well, as they should be working closely together. They should be honest with each other, so cultivate a warm atmosphere. A sense of humour is an advantage in all theatre folk; for those in the wardrobe, who work long hours and must accommodate indecision and changes of mind by the designer, it is essential.

Wardrobe facilities

Costume makers will need appropriate facilities and you should establish whether they will work from home with their own machines or will need you to provide a workroom and equipment. Dance costumes frequently use stretch fabric. This needs either overlocking, or sewing with a stretch stitch or zig zag. Not all sewing machines include a stretch stitch, so check this out in advance. An overlocker might be a necessary investment for those making dance costumes regularly. Such expense must be part of the budget.

Importance of teamwork

Some designers are skilled technicians and can advise on how a costume should be made up; others must rely on the costume maker to realise their design. Four people are involved in the creation of a costume – choreographer, designer, costume maker (or seamstress) and the dancer who will eventually perform in it. They will have strong feelings about the final result and, hopefully, will work in harmony. Understanding is needed of all the participants' concerns. Thus a designer with awareness of the dancers' movements and regard for the budget, a costume maker with respect for the designer and sympathy for the comfort of the dancer, and a dancer with justified trust in both, should produce a happy outcome.

TIPS FOR MAKING DANCE COSTUMES

Outside the stylisation needed for tutus and national dress, costumes for much ballet and modern dance can be based on certain basic shapes and patterns which may be adapted to give different effects. The chief consideration is that the costumes are to be danced in and that means movement! An enthusiastic designer sometimes fails to notice that one dancer spends several seconds upside down in a lift, whilst another slides into the splits – so the several-layered skirt for the former and non-stretch skintight pants for the latter will pose problems. Similarly, after an all-in-one fitting, when costume and bodystocking have been expertly pinned together, the question arises of how the dancer is to get out of her new 'skin' without removing all the precisely placed pins.

Costume maker Joy Duffett cites some common problems with dance costumes and offers some practical tips:

> One of the first things you realise is that resources are always limited, but high expectations still prevail. Dance colleges rightly want their shows to look

professional, and if they specialise in musical theatre, they will expect their show to look like the latest West End musical. The fact that funds are minimal does not always enter their minds, and many items are extremely expensive: special shoes, for instance, may be £30–£40 a pair; the material needed for a circular skirt cannot be skimped, if it is to hang properly, so to make a large number is very costly.

Some producers do not understand that costume makers do not work to opening night; the costumes must be completed at least a week before, to allow them to be danced in and adjusted if necessary.

Costumes must also be made to accommodate quick changes, meaning that loops and buttons will get ripped off in the process, so should be replaced by Velcro. This must be cut and attached in small square-shaped sections rather than one long piece, which will be impossible to align correctly in a rush. Pas de deux costumes should be made in non-slip fabrics, so that the man can get a firm grip on his partner's waist; slippery fabrics can be downright dangerous in lifts and other supported work. Ballet bodices must fit like a second skin so that they move with the body; the body must not move around inside the bodice, so bodices should be fitted much more tightly than normal. To hold a costume in place when the arms are lifted, and to prevent it riding up, it may be necessary to insert a crotch-elastic. This is a piece of wide elastic which is attached underneath the waistband on a non-stretch bodice, and is taken down under the crotch and joined up at the back of the waistband.

Novice costume makers also need to understand that theatre clothes are seen from a distance, so that the fine details of everyday wear are not noticed. Therefore some details are unnecessary: buttonholes, for instance, can be replaced by hooks and bars or Velcro, with a button sewn on the outer layer, as decoration. It is the *effect* which should be aimed for, so costumes for a short run do not need to be made to last.

FABRICS

Effective fabrics for dance costumes are those which move well. Unless a design specifically demands a stiff material, such as net or tarlatan for a tutu, or crisp cotton for a shirt, it is usually better to choose a soft texture, or something stretchy. Jersey, silk, chiffon, georgette and lycra are good choices. These fabrics are effective for skirts, soft trousers, dresses and tops.

Costumes which are to be dyed are best made in natural materials, such as cotton and silk, which 'take' the dye well. It is worth finding sources where these may be bought at reasonable prices. These may be specialist shops, markets or directly from the wholesalers. In London, shops like Borovick or MacCullough and Wallis, markets like the one in the East End's Brick Lane, or the Indian shops in Southall, are excellent starting points. If you cannot find what you want here, then try wholesalers. Renowned for selling a huge variety of natural silks and cottons especially for dyeing, Whaley's in Bradford do an excellent mail order service.

Contact the production department of your nearest dance or theatre company, and ask where they get their materials. They should be pleased to help, and may even be willing to let you hire one or two of their costumes if necessary. Local art colleges may also help regarding fabric suppliers.

BASIC SHAPES

Leotards and all-in-ones are usually purchased nowadays; buy white ones if you wish to dye them. Detailed instructions for making a circular skirt are given on pages 68–9. These can be adapted to create a variety of costumes. A measurement sheet should be prepared for each dancer, comprising: chest, waist, hips, girth, inside leg, outside leg, shoulders, nape to waist, arm length, height, shoe size.

Leotards and all-in-ones

The ideal base for many costumes is the simple leotard. It stretches, does not ride up when arms are lifted and is easily added to. A circular skirt or trousers can be attached and dyed in such a way as to disguise the leotard base, giving the illusion of a one-piece outfit. False sleeves, collars, cuffs, waistbands, shawls and many other accessories can be added. For men, too, a leotard makes a good foundation under trousers or tights. Again the idea is that, when the costume is finished, the leotard will not be obvious, but will serve as a secure foundation garment, in which the dancer can move comfortably and which does not obscure the line of the body.

The all-in-one, also known as catsuit, bodysuit or bodystocking is another staple of the dance wardrobe and one wonders how everyone managed before its invention. The overwhelming advantage of the all-in-one is that it is perfect for displaying line and shape, elements vital in certain ballets.

Costumes designed to be seen from a distance under stage lighting often appear different in colour and texture when viewed up close. In Tetley and Ter Arutunian's *Voluntaries*, the costumes appear white onstage but are in fact mottled. The mottling gives subtle texture and softens the harshness of pure, plain white. Remember that costumes should never be thought of in isolation from the lighting, and that both elements work together towards the desired end.

With the leotard and bodystocking, it is possible to achieve many different effects by the choice of matt or shiny fabric, and the application of various decorative techniques. Pattern and texture are added to a basic plain garment through dyeing, by drawing and painting onto the fabric, spraying and using appliqué. A black sleeveless and knee-length bodystocking could be worn over a red bodystocking with long sleeves, a high neckline and feet to give a total two-colour costume effect. In addition, a top layer can be ripped. Students worked to create the effect of bodies burnt in a fire. Two layers were worn to represent skin, the outer randomly ripped, then the underneath one also ripped, and pulled through the gaps in the top layer. Dye and spray were used to suggest colours of charred flesh, normal and burnt, the end result gory but effective.

Loose fitting tops and bottoms

If choreographic style does not feature line and body shape as crucial elements, as in contact-improvisation, where weight and movement are important, consider how the casual anti-costume look can be maintained in a more formal setting. Loose trousers, either straight-legged or gathered in at the ankle, can look sleek yet weighty if made in a material which hangs well – try different weights of easily dyed cotton jersey – and add a loose fitting top in the same fabric. Variations within this basic shape can add individuality to the dancers whilst maintaining the overall unity –

different sleeves, necklines, trouser lengths or the use of two layers, such as a cropped top over a toning leotard, are possibilities. The quality of the material is crucial: stiff fabric can look boxy, giving the dancers a square and immobile look. To achieve a really loose look, oversized tops can look casually elegant, and men's T-shirts, sweatshirts and vests may be worn by the women.

Inexpensive cotton jersey garments can be found in stores or markets, and can be over-dyed if necessary. The humble pair of leggings lends itself to all sorts of variations, shiny lycra looking totally different from matt cotton, and the various lengths and weights of fabric giving individual effects. Plain black cotton footless leggings make an effective base beneath a skirt, and coloured leggings under a plain black skirt can be a simple alternative if brightness is needed. If you have a large cast of children and funds are short, leggings and T-shirts in various styles and colours are an uncomplicated option. Both garments can be dyed, tie-dyed, painted with fabric paints, appliquéed or sprayed onto to allow individuality, and the decorative techniques could be tried out by older members of the cast.

Skirts

A skirt for dance must hang and move well, its success depending largely on its movement and the way it falls or hangs from the dancer's body. Factors which contribute to this include the quality of fabric, the amount of fabric used, and the way the skirt is cut, then fitted onto the body. Fabric quality should possess a degree of weight, and even delicate material like chiffon should not be so flimsy that it 'flies away', unless this is specifically desired. Skirts which cling to the hips enhance the dancers' line, before falling to knee, calf or ankle and creating gentle movement. All jersey works well in this respect, as does lycra, and to achieve a semi-matt look with the latter, use the wrong side of the shiny lycra fabric.

When deciding on length for a skirt, consider among other things faithfulness to period style, as well as line and movement. Some lengths flatter more than others, as do the particular placing, fitting and style of waistline and waistband. Waistlines in costume, just as in fashion, vary enormously and placement may give a hint of style and period to a broadly 'abstract' costume.

Hemlines may be straight or shaped, and include those which dip slightly at the back and those in an asymmetrical style. Cutting the lengths should be done late in the creative process, after skirts cut on the bias have been hung up to allow them to drop, stretching slightly in length. If they are to be worn for rehearsals, long skirts should be trimmed so that the dancers will not trip, but the final length should be left until near to the first performance. Remember that once it has been cut, you cannot add to it again, so all trimming should be done very carefully.

Tutus

If a tutu is your choice of costume, give thought to the exact look you want, and find an expert costume maker – you can never bluff an audience over a tutu – the experts will know! Or contact your nearest ballet company or vocational school, and ask about hiring some of theirs. It may be assumed that tutus are all stiff, frilly and identical, but like any costume, the tutu has a history and has been subject to changes in style. Consider the long Romantic tutu and the short Classical one. The former in fact can vary in length from design to design, and the latter may appear as a longer, floppy Russian style, a hooped 'plate-topped' one or a 'powder puff'. Designers have

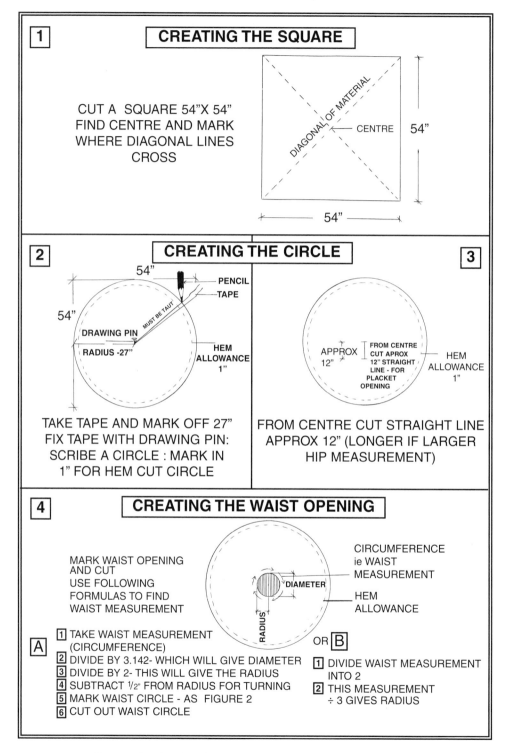

Pattern for circular skirt © David Dean, redrawn for this book

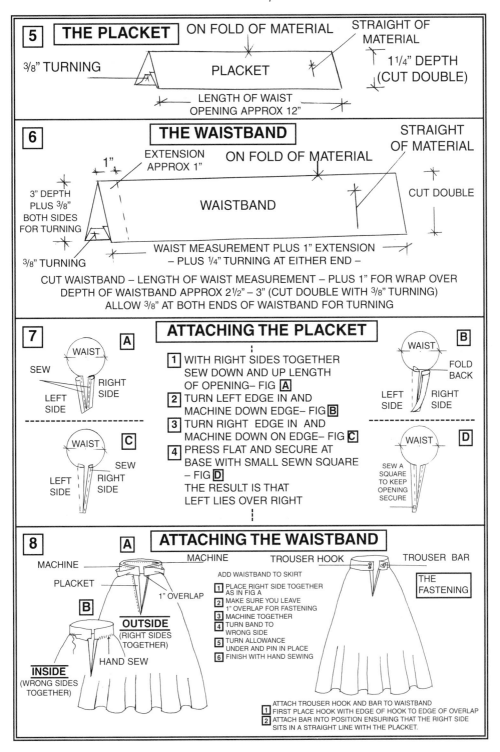

5 **THE PLACKET** ON FOLD OF MATERIAL STRAIGHT OF MATERIAL

3/8" TURNING PLACKET 1¼" DEPTH (CUT DOUBLE)

LENGTH OF WAIST OPENING APPROX 12"

6 **THE WAISTBAND** STRAIGHT OF MATERIAL

1" EXTENSION APPROX 1" ON FOLD OF MATERIAL

3" DEPTH PLUS 3/8" BOTH SIDES FOR TURNING WAISTBAND CUT DOUBLE

3/8" TURNING WAIST MEASUREMENT PLUS 1" EXTENSION – PLUS ¼" TURNING AT EITHER END –

CUT WAISTBAND – LENGTH OF WAIST MEASUREMENT – PLUS 1" FOR WRAP OVER
DEPTH OF WAISTBAND APPROX 2½" – 3" (CUT DOUBLE WITH 3/8" TURNING)
ALLOW 3/8" AT BOTH ENDS OF WAISTBAND FOR TURNING

7 **A** **ATTACHING THE PLACKET** **B**

WAIST SEW LEFT SIDE RIGHT SIDE

WAIST FOLD BACK LEFT SIDE RIGHT SIDE

1 WITH RIGHT SIDES TOGETHER SEW DOWN AND UP LENGTH OF OPENING– FIG **A**
2 TURN LEFT EDGE IN AND MACHINE DOWN EDGE– FIG **B**
3 TURN RIGHT EDGE IN AND MACHINE DOWN ON EDGE– FIG **C**
4 PRESS FLAT AND SECURE AT BASE WITH SMALL SEWN SQUARE – FIG **D**
THE RESULT IS THAT LEFT LIES OVER RIGHT

C WAIST LEFT SIDE RIGHT SIDE SEW

D WAIST SEW A SQUARE TO KEEP OPENING SECURE

8 **A** **ATTACHING THE WAISTBAND**

MACHINE MACHINE TROUSER HOOK TROUSER BAR
PLACKET 1" OVERLAP THE FASTENING

ADD WAISTBAND TO SKIRT
1 PLACE RIGHT SIDE TOGETHER AS IN FIG A
2 MAKE SURE YOU LEAVE 1" OVERLAP FOR FASTENING
3 MACHINE TOGETHER
4 TURN BAND TO WRONG SIDE
5 TURN ALLOWANCE UNDER AND PIN IN PLACE
6 FINISH WITH HAND SEWING

B OUTSIDE (RIGHT SIDES TOGETHER) HAND SEW
INSIDE (WRONG SIDES TOGETHER)

ATTACH TROUSER HOOK AND BAR TO WAISTBAND
1 FIRST PLACE HOOK WITH EDGE OF HOOK TO EDGE OF OVERLAP
2 ATTACH BAR INTO POSITION ENSURING THAT THE RIGHT SIDE SITS IN A STRAIGHT LINE WITH THE PLACKET.

also created various radical versions, such as Thomas O'Neil's asymmetrical tutu for MacMillan's *The Poltroon* (1972) and in Derek Deane's *Alice in Wonderland* (1994) for English National Ballet, Sue Blane designed flat, square tutus to represent the playing card characters.

HAIR AND HEADWEAR

The head is the heaviest part of the body and the dancer needs to be able to move it with complete freedom, for both artistic and safety purposes. Any heavy, bulky or insecurely fixed item on the head can upset the dancer's balance, causing a hazard for the dancer and others, and it may make a *pirouette* or other fast turn impossible. This applies to hair as well as headdresses and hats.

Hair is an element of design and should be integrated with the movement. Novice designers for dance often have elaborate ideas for headgear and hair, which are occasionally scrapped after rehearsals.

Ballet traditionally evokes visions of classical hairdos and headdresses for the women, which take skill to get exactly right. The three main factors are authenticity, the correct 'look' for the work, and the translation of this onto the actual dancer, with her own individual hair length, shape of head, length of neck and facial bone structure.

Modern dance may allow for 'everyday' hairstyles; short cropped styles shape the head and pose no problems of styling or weight, although it may be difficult to attach a headdress to very short hair. Longer styles may be sleeked back from the face and arranged in various ways; ponytails (tied high or low on the crown), plaits or bunches. If double work is involved, a ponytail might hit the man in the face, so should be considered carefully. The choreography might make it appropriate to have long hair simply hanging down round the face, in which case it should include swings of the head, allowing the dancer to swing the hair off the face!

A headdress can be a simple circlet of flowers. The precise placement of the headdress is crucial – it should not look as if it is plonked on, or perching like a bird on a nest. The whole head should look neat, sleek, elegant and small, and remain that way throughout fast turns, jumps and lifts.

With larger, more elaborate and unwieldy headdresses, even more care must be taken. In these cases, there may be the additional consideration of further width and height needed around the head. This will certainly affect partner work, and possibly even other dancers in close proximity. Will the extra height added to dancers permit them to enter through a stage doorway, or will they need to duck in order to get through? The same applies to the width – will they get stuck?

The eye is always drawn to the head area; it is a focal point, and if it looks wrong or out of proportion it can ruin an otherwise harmonious effect.

COLOUR

The use of colour in costume and sets is one of the most important and exciting aspects of theatre design. When colour from lighting is also added, the combined effect can be the most powerful visual statement of the whole enterprise. Artists understand this, but dancers occasionally have a somewhat limited approach to the use of colour, sticking to stereotyped ideas of what suits them! One of the first attitudes a designer will encounter is that dancers want, above all, to look slim, no, thin, and every prospective costume will be judged not for its imaginativeness, or its contribution to the overall effect, but on whether it makes them look fat! Rest assured that the only colour considered acceptable will be black. Navy might just pass the test, but the suggestion of white is likely to cause hysterics, as is yellow. However, it is often not the actual colour which causes a costume to be unflattering or not – and brilliant white shiny lycra under open white stage lighting can look hideous – but other factors such as shade, texture and placement.

Beware of the effect of large expanses of 'solid' colour on a body, particularly if the colour is bright or garish. This causes the shape to appear 'static' and in a block. Bought leotards, tights and all-in-ones can look utilitarian, particularly in shiny lycra. Think of a dance school uniform, royal blue or burgundy leotards or catsuits, for instance; serviceable, anonymous, no-nonsense, and absolutely appropriate for class or rehearsal. When it comes to making an artistic statement in costume terms, these need to be transformed or they will look mundane.

It is important to consider the lighting when selecting colours. Certain combinations of colour work together better than others. Let's say you want red and blue costumes, and think that red and blue colours in the sidelights will pick them up nicely. Well, the red in the light would enhance the red in the costumes, and likewise the blue, but when the blue light hits the red costume, and vice versa, you'd get, yes, purple! Maybe purple is what you want, but if it is not, be careful how you combine the colours. Of course, the lighting designer might decide to use open white light (no colour) on the red and blue designs, an option sometimes necessary when there are simply too many colours in a work to bring all of them out. Toning warm, or toning cool colours light well: warm shades of yellow, orange, gold, tan, russet, red and brown look beautiful when lit in corresponding colours. Cool aquamarine, blue, turquoise, kingfisher and jade work well together, and purple or mauve, with predominantly blue or pink tones are also easy to light.

Dyeing

Basic dyeing is fun and it is worth knowing a few simple techniques. If you have the know-how and facilities to dye fabric, dyeing can be the most creative way of achieving colours and effects. Searching for coloured material to buy, in the exact shade you require, is a laborious and occasionally fruitless task. By mixing dyes, you can produce a huge range of colours, and shade, patch and tie-dye to achieve interest and texture. Shading involves grading the depth of colour over a garment: for example, a skirt may be pale green at the waist, shading through mid to dark green at the hemline. As well as giving texture, shading can emphasise or minimise a part of the dancer's body. On the principle that light colours stand out and darker colours recede, a dancer of uneven proportions could be balanced by making a top darker and the bottom lighter, or vice versa. Shading can also unify a costume with top and bottom in different colours, by blending round the middle, thus avoiding the unflattering effect of cutting the body in half at the waist.

There are basic rules to successful dyeing. Firstly, there must be no doubt that the fabric will take the dye. Natural fabrics such as cotton and silk absorb dye easily and give a true colour when dyed from white or natural. Synthetic fabrics, such as polyester, take dye less well, becoming a pale or mid colour, but not a dark or rich shade. Nylon lycra dyes well with hot-water dye, made by Dylon in the UK, and available in small round tubs of powder. Machine or cold-water dyes will not work on lycra. Cotton lycra works like a synthetic; it can be difficult to achieve a dark colour and sometimes several dippings are needed to strengthen and deepen the original shade. The colour of the fabric at the start will, of course, affect the end result.

Stripping

You cannot dye a dark colour to a paler one, but it may be possible to strip colour out of a fabric by using a special solution. In the UK this is called PreDye. It is a powder which, when dissolved in boiling water, acts as a kind of bleach, but without destroying the fabric. It is worth experimenting with stripping. Fast-dyed colour cannot be removed, and one cannot always tell whether a fabric can be successfully stripped; trial and error are the only way. PreDye must be used in a well-ventilated area, as it is extremely strong smelling, and it should not be inhaled – follow the instructions on the packet.

After stripping, the garment is a colour anywhere from white, if it was dyed originally from white, through shades of cream and natural, to a dull yellow-orange if all the dye cannot be removed. These shades of off-white are suitable for redyeing. However, if the result of stripping leaves the fabric a yellow-orange, it will be impossible to redye it to a very pale shade such as ice-blue.

Dyeing for beginners

Here is a guide to simple techniques which work with minimal resources. I started with a few leotards that needed brightening, a gas stove, large pan, stirrer and plastic washing-up bowl. These are the basics, and yes, dyeing does make a mess, but ordinary household cleaners effectively remove traces of dye from worktops.

Start with a few experiments before tackling an actual garment. Find several pieces of material, no bigger than 25cm (10in.) square. These should fit easily in your pan when wet, otherwise they will not stay submerged in the dye and may also overhang dangerously near the flame of a gas cooker. Choose fabrics identical or similar to those you will want to dye for costumes – ideally, white or pale coloured pure cotton, silk, nylon lycra, cotton lycra and an obvious synthetic. This could be a mix of polyester and cotton, or polyester chiffon.

1 First, soak all the pieces in plain water until they are fully wet.
2 The dye to use is a small tub of hot-water dye, and you need table salt as a fixative. Into a separate container tip about half the contents of the dye tub, plus a few teaspoonfuls of salt. Add boiling water and stir until dissolved. I use a long metal salad server for stirring.
3 Pour this mixture into the dyeing pan, and add hot water until the pan is two thirds full. Put it on the heat, and stir further.
4 Now add one of the pieces to be dyed, turn the heat down to simmering point and stir. The mixture should be kept at boiling point for as long as it takes for the fabric to absorb the colour. You may be surprised how quickly this happens with a pure fabric. The longer you leave the fabric simmering in the pan, the stronger the colour will be, up to the limit of the dye used. The instructions on the dye tin

suggest twenty minutes as the maximum time for the colour to take. In your experiment, try leaving pieces of the same fabric for different lengths of time and observe the results. Also notice how each type of fabric reacts differently to the dye. This process of trial and error is the best way to gain familiarity with dyeing and gaining confidence to tackle an actual garment. Remember, the worst that can happen is that you don't like the new colour after all, and this can be rectified by using the PreDye already mentioned, which will take it back to its original shade.

5   When you have achieved the colour you want, carefully remove the material from the pan and rinse thoroughly. Be aware that the colour appears several shades darker when wet. Spin dry the fabric and hang to dry. Before emptying the dye away, test dry a patch of the dyed fabric using an iron or a hairdryer. This will show the final colour when completely dry. If it is too pale, simply wet it and put it back in the pan for a while longer.

Basically, equipment needed for hot-water dyeing and shading is simply a container large enough to hold the fabric, which can keep water at boiling point for the length of time needed for the dye to take.

The above method of dyeing will only work for small garments. If you are going to dye anything larger than a single all-in-one, you need a washboiler and a washing machine. These two pieces of equipment will enable you to do a considerable amount of effective dyeing.

Using a washing machine   The washing machine needs to be a front-loader, as the process does not work in a top-loader, and an ordinary household front-loader is fine – you do not need a special programme. Dylon make dye specifically for machine-dyeing, and all you need to do is follow the instructions on the packet. However, it only works on pure fabrics such as cotton, and I prefer to dye delicate silks in the washboiler. The machine is ideal for larger amounts of pure cotton fabric, which needs dyeing to an even 'solid' colour. If you have, say, several dresses to dye, made out of heavy cotton jersey, machine dyeing is ideal, as the sheer weight of the wet material can prove unwieldy in a washboiler. However, the machine will not shade, patch or tie-dye and it is a little harder to experiment, as you cannot stop the machine's cycle to see how it's doing.

The first time you dye in a machine, you may wonder if you are doing it right. You must tip the dye powder into the drum, and get it into the holes in the side. This involves turning the drum in a circular fashion and patting the powder down with a flat spoon into the holes. Then a considerable quantity of salt needs to go in as a fixative. I rarely manage to get all the powder into the holes, and am always concerned that the wet fabric is going to pick up extra colour from the remaining dye. However, once the cycle gets going it somehow comes out alright!

You need to judge how much dye you will need, relative to the amount of fabric to be dyed, and the colour you want. Two or more dyeings are sometimes needed for a deep colour. Colours can be mixed, and paler or darker versions of the same shade can be used on individual garments to give unity, but not uniformity to a group of costumes. One advantage of machine dyeing is that rinsing and spinning are done for you, enabling hot-water and machine dyeing to be done simultaneously if time is limited.

Home dyeing with washboiler and washing machine (PHOTO: *author*)

Using a washboiler Anything other than a pure fabric (including lycra which contains man-made fibres) needs to be dyed in a washboiler. They are ideal for hot water dyeing, and for shade and patch effects. They come in several sizes and are relatively inexpensive when you consider the amount of use to which they will be put. They are definitely a worthwhile investment if you are dyeing costumes regularly.

They work in a similar way to a pan on a gas cooker, except that they are larger and electric, making them safer and more comfortable to use. The same hot-water dyes are used, with salt as fixative. Shade dyeing can be done in a washboiler as follows:

1 First dye the entire garment in the palest shade of the colour you want, to ensure a uniform base throughout. Take the garment carefully out of the boiler and leave in a plastic bowl.
2 Add more dye to the mixture in the boiler to achieve the next darker shade you want, then place only the area to be shaded, back in the water, ensuring that the palest area does not come into contact with the darker dye. This is the hardest part; keeping the paler areas out of the water whilst the deeper colour takes.

3 The process is repeated with each darker shade desired. To avoid a line at the point each darker shade begins, allow the darker colour to bleed gradually into the lighter by holding the garment up.

When dyeing is complete always ensure that the washboiler is carefully cleaned out and rinsed, or you may leave traces of colour which run into your next dyeing job.

DECORATIVE TECHNIQUES

Fabric pens
Fabric pens can be used to draw directly onto the garment. Use waterproof ones obtainable in most art shops. If the costume is made of stretch material, it should always be worn whilst the drawing takes place. Use the dancer who will eventually wear the costume, or someone of approximately the same size. This is because the fabric stretches on the body, and the size and precise placement of the design cannot be gauged accurately without the correct amount of stretch to work on.

All-in-ones described on page 76, 'Greek' drapes and patterns drawn with fabric pens (PHOTO: *Chris Davies*)

David Dean advises on use of fabric pens for Royal Academy of Dancing College workshop costumes (PHOTO: *Chris Davies*)

Before attacking a carefully made garment with a fabric pen, work out the design on paper and choose colours. It should also be decided whereabouts on the body each part of the design is to go. Is the design going over the hips, the shoulders or down one leg? Fabric pens are not especially cheap but, given the effects they can achieve and the alternatives, they are well worth the expense. For example, a suggestion of Ancient Greece was needed for one set of costumes; Greek tunics, or chitons, could have been used but they require a great deal of material draped about the body. Clean lines were indicated by the choreography, so a tunic seemed too bulky. Eventually, it was decided to draw the drapes onto an all-in-one base using a Greek key design as decoration. The solution proved extremely effective, combining the sculptural line with the suggestion of antiquity. See illustration on page 75.

Appliqué

The use of appliqué is a simple way to add design and texture to a costume. A design can be drawn onto pale material with fabric pens, then cut out and stitched or glued onto a garment. When using appliqué on a stretchy costume, stretch fabric must also be used for the appliqué. An illustration is shown below.

Spraying

Striking effects can be achieved with the skilled use of the humble can of car spray paint and a stencil. Spraying is normally the final effect to be added to a costume and is done after dyeing and finishing off. The use of patterns or shading adds texture, decoration or colour and, when expertly done, makes the difference between a professional and an amateur look. Skill is needed in making a stencil, practice and patience in handling the spray can, and sensitivity with the nozzle! Standing too close to the garment, or giving too swift or abrupt a press on the nozzle, will result in a big squirt of spray, splat, in a solid patch on the fabric. You are aiming for a

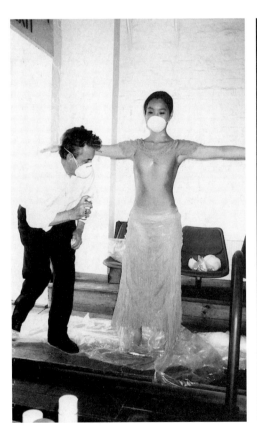

Shading a costume with spray – note open door, nose masks and polythene sheeting beneath the costume to keep spray off skin (PHOTO: *author*)

All-in-one with spray and appliqué in 'metallic' fabric (PHOTO: *Tony King*)

drizzle of paint giving a subtle shadow, which can be graduated in terms of heaviness and density of colour. This is particularly appropriate when spraying directly onto a costume with a stencil, to give colour shading or blending. Just as with dyeing, spray shading can sculpt and blend. Dye and spray can be used in combination, with the spraying always last.

To shade effectively round the waist or hips, the dancer must wear the costume whilst it is being done. To ensure that the spray does not get onto the skin, polythene or plastic bags should be placed underneath the costume and should cover arms, legs and neck. For a long spraying session, both the person doing the spraying and the dancer being sprayed should wear a protective mask over the nose. The spray is not dangerous, but it can give you a headache, so make sure all the windows are wide open!

MAKE UP

Make-up is another part of design. A dancer's make-up will depend on the venue, the lighting and the distance of the audience. Where no special make-up is required by the designer, the aim will be to enhance the individual's face and make it clearly visible from a distance. As in everyday make-up, the features should be evident, not the 'slap'! The features should be 'opened out' to be seen from afar, with the space between eyebrows and eyes evident and the bone structure emphasised. Eyes and lips should be clearly delineated in as natural a fashion as possible, taking care with colour. The stronger the stage lighting, and the further away the audience, the bolder the make-up. False eyelashes and 'tramlines' round the eyes in greasepaint are a thing of the past, with new cosmetics and techniques achieving the same results by different means. Many dance performances take place in smaller settings with the audience close to the stage, and a heavy day make-up may suffice, but the presence of stage lighting bleaches the skin, necessitating more blusher and stronger eyes and lips. Fashion colours, like very dark plummy lipsticks or very pale ones, will be used only in character or 'fashion' works. A 'basic' face needs more natural colours for lips, eyes and skin.

Children need only mascara, a little eyeshadow and lipstick, with optional pencil for eyelines or brows. Men and boys will need a more brown shade for lips.

9. Lighting

Even if they would not know a gobo from a grelco, or a shin-buster from a scroller, most dance audiences welcome effective lighting and appreciate how it enhances the overall result. Today's public has been exposed to extravagant lighting effects in clubs, rock concerts and musicals, and expectations are greater than they were twenty years ago.

With the trend of dance design towards the abandonment of painted backcloths in favour of construction-based sets or a bare stage, lighting has assumed a greater importance in the overall design concept. It has also been enhanced by the talents of lighting designers such as Jean Rosenthal, John B. Read and Jennifer Tipton, who have collaborated with some of the most innovative and influential choreographers and designers.

WHAT IS YOUR SITUATION?

Groups will find themselves in one of three situations:

1 Lighting equipment and personnel will be exclusively those of the venue. If the venue provides equipment, what type is it, how much, and is it included in the hiring price? Who will design the rig and operate it – staff belonging to the hall, the visiting company, or a mixture of both? Are the venue's staff included in the hiring price? What hours are the stage and technicians available, before and during the show?
2 Lighting equipment and personnel will be exclusively those of the dance company. In this case there are no facilities at the venue, let's say a gymnasium. If a group has its own lights and technician, check electrical power well in advance to ensure it is sufficient to take the incoming equipment. This can be assessed by a qualified theatre technician or electrician. If the dance group itself has no facilities, then the show should be done in the normal everyday lighting of the venue, or with a designer/technician and equipment brought in from outside.
3 Lighting equipment and personnel will be a mixture of both. In this case all that is needed is communication, communication, communication!

Groups which tour with their own equipment obviously need transport as well as technical implementation, meaning a van and driver.

Hire or borrow?
Once the basics are established, the next stage is to discuss the project with the lighting designer. The designer decides, according to the show's requirements, the equipment already *in situ* and the funds available, if extra lights or other equipment are needed. These could be hired, or possibly borrowed. Groups might do a deal,

lending out a couple of fresnels in exchange for some extra cable and a strobe, and it goes without saying that borrowed equipment should be scrupulously cared for, and returned on schedule. Lighting is costly, and impecunious groups reliant on limited resources can be badly affected by irresponsibility in the care of equipment and its return. Hire charges are quite competitive so it is customary to obtain quotes from a number of firms, and it may also be possible to get a good deal in return for free advertising in the programme.

RESOURCES

Resources to be budgeted for are as follows:

- lighting designer
- technician(s)
- the venue's equipment
- any extra items to be hired in or borrowed.

A skilled lighting designer will utilise human, technical and financial resources to maximum effect. You should establish at the earliest opportunity who and what will be available at the venue on the night of performance and during the production period beforehand. Unlike other staging operations, lighting cannot be rehearsed in isolation, weeks in advance, nor tried out in a different location. Only when all other aspects of staging are in place can the lighting be organised. There is less time available for experimenting with lighting than for other staging aspects, because of the high cost of stage time.

Everything must work harmoniously. This means the lighting designer, the stage manager, the technician and equipment. One element not up to scratch will undermine the entire process. A first-class rig and technician will not conceal an unimaginative or inappropriate design; an excellent lighting design will not be evident if the Stage Manager cues inaccurately; and if faulty or inadequately serviced equipment causes a computerised lighting board to crash in mid-show, then everybody's work is wasted!

How many people do you need?
Your group's personnel and finances will determine how many people are involved in lighting. Only a few companies have sufficient funding for a full-time technician, and only those with permanent residence in a theatre work regularly with the same technical staff. Other groups may have their own lighting resources in addition those of the venue, or may be totally dependent on the facilities and personnel of each individual hall and theatre.

What needs to be done?
To get an idea of the number of people needed, and with what skills, let's look at what lighting involves. It can then be decided whom you need and can afford, and whether some jobs could be 'doubled up' and undertaken by one person.
Someone needs to:

- design the rig
- order the equipment

- put up, cable and focus the lights
- plot each state
- cue the changes
- operate the lighting board
- remove and return equipment at the end of the performance, or run.

DANCE LIGHTING

Lighting for dance differs from lighting for drama. This affects the type of lighting needed and its placement. In dance, the visibility and clarity of the movement are crucial, whereas, in drama, the faces are more important. A three-dimensional effect is needed to make the figures and movements stand out from their surroundings and the dancers' bodies are approached as if they were sculpture. Side lighting is used for modelling the bodies, with top light from overhead or at a slight angle. Back light is used for deep saturated colour. Front lighting tends to flatten out the bodies, but is used for lighting the faces.

WHAT CAN LIGHT DO?

In addition to making the dancers visible and sculpting the bodies and limbs, what else can good dance lighting contribute?

- lighting creates mood and atmosphere
- lighting may suggest time and place
- lighting can focus the audience's attention on a specific part of the action.

Cold and warm states
The colour, intensity, placement and timing of the lights are the means by which effects are created. Cold and warm states, colour washes and 'specials' can be used to create these effects. Cold and warm states are the basic lighting states to which 'specials' may be added.

'Cold' and 'warm' refer to the predominance of cool or warm colours, and may correspond to the emotional feeling of the work or tones in costume and set. A colour wash does exactly what its name suggests, 'washing' the space with colour.

A BASIC DANCE RIG

A basic dance rig can consist of the following:

- three levels of side lights
- two (minimum) or more (preferably) toplights, depending on funds available
- backlights
- front-of-house lights – these are the least important
- it is also common for dance to use pipe-ends – pipe is the American term for lighting bar, and pipe-ends are simply lights placed at the extreme ends of the bars to give cross light.

Functions of cross lighting

Light beams which cross the stage from side lights or pipe-ends are responsible for creating the three-dimensional look. Booms (stands) allow lights to be hung from floor level upwards and to light the body from different angles. Those nearest the floor are known as 'shin-busters'.

Planning the rig

Having decided on the budget, the designer then plans the rig. The rig is the plan of what lights to use and where to put them (see lighting rig plan on page 87). They can be hung overhead on bars or girders, and mounted on booms or stands in the wings and in the audience area (as front-of-house lights, or FOHs, as they are called). FOHs may be focused onto the stage or may provide illumination for the auditorium itself, if it is in a 'converted' space. It is worth remembering that in venues without facilities, it will be necessary to bring in equipment on which to hang the lights.

The other major factor in deciding the rig is, or course, the show itself. Before the final lighting plan is drawn up and equipment ordered, the lighting designer will have been to rehearsals and spoken with the choreographer and designer. An idea of how the work should look will begin to emerge and the lighting designer will start to make decisions about lighting plans. However, these will not be finalised until the technical rehearsal onstage, when all the staging elements are in place. Lighting states may be determined by many factors: the emotional or dramatic development of a work; the shift from many dancers onstage to a soloist; the need to isolate a specific part of the action or to accommodate a scene change in a longer piece.

GENERAL COVER AND SELECTIVE LIGHT SOURCES

A work using a large number of dancers covering the entire stage may need more general, overall lighting cover than one which seeks to isolate one or more dancers. The latter will call for a selective light source that will pick out only the area in which the dancer is moving, or will highlight small, subtle movements.

Some commonly used lights

It is worth being able to identify and understand the basic functions of commonly used lights.

A fresnel is used for a wash of colour. It has a stepped lens which diffuses the light, and a round beam which is shaped by a barndoor. This is a device made up of four shutters, which is attached to the front of the light.

Profile spots come in various sizes but always have a smooth lens, giving a sharp edge to the light. Their round beams are shaped by internal shutters and they can accommodate a gobo.

Floods are generally, nowadays, only used in banks of colour to light a white cyc, most commonly from above but also from below.

A par can, popularly used in rock concerts, gives a very bright, punchy light. It has

Portable lighting stand at Blitz '96
(PHOTO: *author*)

three types of beam available, narrow, medium or wide. These are determined by the choice of lamp (bulb). It has an oval shaped beam and is the best choice for backlight when using very deep colours.

A PC is similar to a fresnel. It has a prismed lens which gives a slightly harder edge to the light, and its beam is shaped by a barndoor.

'Specials'
'Specials' (special effects) are individual pools of light over and above the basic states. They may light the dancers, the set or the floor, and are generally used sparingly.
Additional lighting effects include the following:

Strobe A rapidly flashing lantern under which action appears to be frozen. It is popular in discos. In a public performance, the presence of a strobe effect must be notified in the programme, as it can sometimes cause an epileptic fit in those who are susceptible.

UV This is an ultra-violet light, which is used in a blackout to pick out white and specially treated materials which fluoresce and make them appear to glow. A fun effect. A UV light can also cover a multitude of sins in the choreography or dancing!

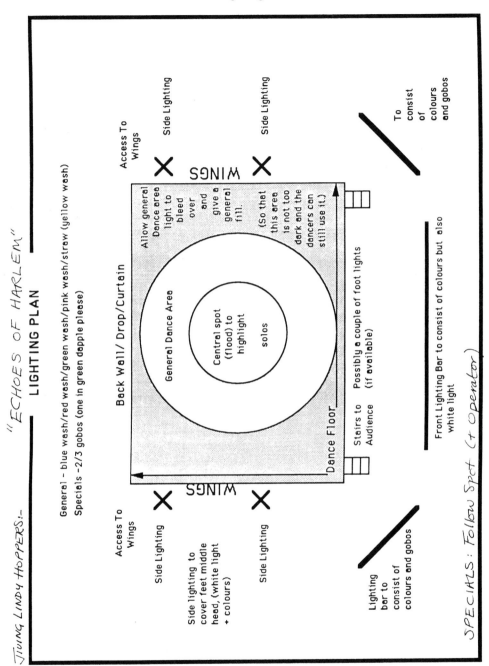

Jiving Lindy Hoppers' lighting plan for Echoes of Harlem

JIVING LINDY HOPPERS

Lighting States: "Echoes of Harlem"

Lighting State No.	Description
1	PRE-SET - general low light (natural colours)
2	BRIGHT STATE - using RED as a highlight
3	BLUE WASH - (as base) and general fill
4	BREAK UP GOBO - Straw/Yellow wash and general fill
5	Ideally just FOLLOW SPOT (If not available, a general flood on central area from above).
6	GREEN & BLUE WASHES and general fill (quite bright)
7	WHITE LIGHT from above to hight central area and general fill with washes
8	BRIGHT STATE - using all colours
9	GREEN DAPPLE GOBO & GREEN WASH to fill and touch of white light
10	As 9 plus BLUES & REDS to become a bright state
11	As 10 but not as bright
12	BLUE WASH (as base) and MEDIUM FLASHING of alternate colours
13	FOLLOW SPOT (General wash in Straw/Yellow)
14	BRIGHT STATE - using reds/yellows/blues etc.
15	RED WASH and general fill
16	STRAW/YELLOW WASH and touch of white light
17	BRIGHT STATE - using all colours
18	As 17
19	BLACKOUT
General:	Side Lighting to enhance the above states

Glitter (or mirror) ball Every dance hall has a glitter ball which rotates, sending winking rays of light round the room.

Gobo A gobo is a metal plate, with a design cut out like a stencil. It is slotted into the front of a profile spot lamp. Its two main uses are to throw a design, such as a window, or dappled effect, onto stage, floor or backcloth, or to break up the light and add texture.

A chase effect This is a series of rapidly changing, pulsing lights in a set or random sequence, an effect often found in discos.

Rope lights These are a series of small individual coloured lamps embedded in a cable.

Colour wheel This is fixed to the front of a light and rotates on electronic signal to place a different colour in front of the beam

SOME BASIC LIGHTING IDEAS

Here are some possibilities that are easy to create:

- stage 'moonlight' or 'sunset' suggests time and gives atmosphere
- a gobo may evoke clouds, or sunlight through trees, indicating place
- lighting which builds slowly, over several minutes, can hint at dawn and sunrise
- in a piece involving dramatic conflict, red lighting may enhance the angry atmosphere
- an 'interior' nightclub scene can be suggested by several different coloured lights against a dimly-lit setting.

And so on.

EXAMPLE: LIGHTING A CONVERTED DANCE STUDIO

A large bare studio had to be converted into a theatre setting for the Royal Academy of Dancing College's Workshop performances, with around fifteen short dances. This was a challenge which Chris Davey, a lighting designer, undertook for a number of very successful years, during which time he learned how to make the most of the opportunities and limitations afforded by the situation. Any studio like this needs to have sufficient electrical output to take stage lighting. This must be assessed by a qualified electrician. The studio ceiling needs to have sufficient height if lights are to be hung.

Chris Davey's comments are of service to anyone considering transforming a studio into a theatre space, on a temporary basis.

With a basic studio setting, and the need to make each piece look as individual as possible, the main tools I had were colour, and a number of keen students available to change gels in the sidelights between numbers. I had to ensure that the highest side lights could be reached by 5ft 2in dance students, and then make everything else multi-purpose. The black cyc available focused emphasis on the bodies and floor, so although there are more possibilities with a white cyc, at least with black I didn't have to light the backcloth, so the rig could be used for other things. The pale brown of the maple floor tended to dominate the dancers, so I found ways to 'lose' it, using blues to dull its effect. The need for variety resulted in subtle use of colours, some light pastel and other thicker colours on top of the warm and cool states.

Royal Academy of Dance
Workshop 1995
Lighting Design:- David Plater

KEY

SYMBOL

LANTERN TYPE   QUANTITY

Sil 30 1K

Leko 6 x 22 1K

Prelude 28 \ 40 650W

Parcan CP62 1K

Cantata PC 1.2K

1K Fresnel

Minuette Fresnel 650W

Coda Flood 500W

Rainbow Colour Scroller

**** Lighting Board Sirius 48****

SCROLLERS

FRAME NUMBER	GEL NO	COLOUR
FRAME ONE	#382	CONGO BLUE
FRAME TWO	L200	CORRECTION BLUE
FRAME THREE	L204	FULL C.T. ORANGE
FRAME FOUR	#21	GOLDEN AMBER
FRAME FIVE	#22	DEEP AMBER
FRAME SIX	#19	FIRE
FRAME SEVEN	L119	DARK BLUE
FRAME EIGHT	L120	DEEP BLUE
FRAME NINE	L164	FLAME RED
FRAME TEN	#00	CLEAR
FRAME ELEVEN	L106	PRIMARY RED
FRAME TWELVE	#385	ROYAL BLUE
FRAME THIRTEEN	L139	PRIMARY GREEN
FRAME FOURTEEN	L116	MED BLUE-GREEN
FRAME FIFTEEN	L127	SMOKEY PINK
FRAME SIXTEEN	L156	CHOCOLATE

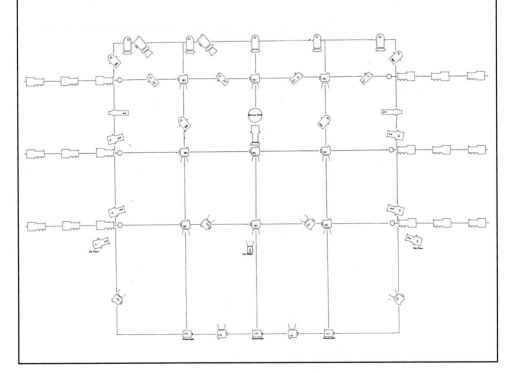

RAD lighting plan including use of scrollers

Chris observed that black legs are often preferable for masking. Black absorbs light and reduces the amount of spill after the light beam has usefully lit the dancer, an important point when remembering that ideally the beam only hits the person or object intended, yet in reality it continues beyond this point of focus.

David Plater, who took over from Chris commented on the value of having students to change colour gels, 'In the professional theatre, it would be too expensive to hire stage staff for this, and so scrollers would need to be used with each light to give the same effect.'

Scrollers are automatic colour changers which allow the colours to be changed 'live' – that is, whilst the light is on. Scrollers can be used with onstage lights which cannot be reached between dances except by ladder. Scrollers were used as part of the lighting which transformed one dance from a serviceable fun number, to a glamorous and sophisticated jazz finale. The dancers wore matt black leotards, tights and jazz shoes with a single gold, elbow-length evening glove and a gold choker. Everyone wanted a theatrical look and David gave them this, and more! A mirror ball turned throughout the piece, with the dancers lit only by shin-busters in open white (no colour). The slight upward angle of these lights meant that no light spilled onto the floor, and the open white enhanced the clean lines of the black costumes. Continuously changing colours were provided by a scroller on a backlight which threw colour onto the floor. The use of a smoke gun onstage, during the blackout preceding the dance, meant that 'changing coloured smoke' rose and hung in the air above the dancers' heads. Not only was the whole stage full of texture and colour, but the dancers stood out sometimes in silhouette, at other times moving into and out of coloured lightbeams, which enhanced their shapes and emphasised the sculptural look of their movements.

10. Stage Management

The Stage Manager is responsible for everything that happens onstage and backstage. He or she runs the show, co-ordinates the performers with the stage crew and other technical departments, and with front-of-house staff. He must understand all the technical and artistic elements which go into a production and have the authority and management skills to work alongside the director, choreographer, musical director and lighting designer. Your production will be entrusted to the Stage Manager, who will become as familiar and as involved with your work as you are. The Stage Manager's word is final. A small group may have only one person to stage manage, design and rig the lighting, drive the van, lay the floor and look after the dancers.

SPECIAL REQUIREMENTS FOR DANCE

In drama, all moves, entrances and exits are cued by the Stage Manager, whereas in dance these are part of the choreography. Intricate and speedy movements into and out of the wings affect the placing of stage masking, side lights, and cabling, which must not obstruct the dancers' path. Annie Lincoln of English National Ballet explains that a key feature of stage managing dance is the speed at which the dancers move on and offstage, making entrances and exits much more complex than those in straight theatre. Dancers' wellbeing requires that drinking water is on hand to offset dehydration; a 'magic box' is kept in the wings, containing first-aid items, arnica for bruises, throat sweets and tissues, as well as safety-pins and wig-repair.

RUNNING THE SHOW AND CUEING

The Stage Manager runs the show and delivers the lighting and sound cues. 'Being on the book', as it is called, is a crucially significant job; cueing demands skill, sensitivity, patience, concentration and a cool head.

Who decides the cues?
What does this involve, how does the person cueing know where the cues should come, and who decides where they should come? In drama the play's script is the basis, and in an opera or musical, the composer's score. Against this background the light and sound cues are organised – the script or score is the 'book' on which the cues, decided by the lighting and sound designers, will be marked by the Stage Manager. This process is known as 'blocking', and the 'book' will be followed during the course of the show. The lighting and sound are as important to the end result as the choreography and performance, and the cues are planned in close collaboration with the choreographer and designer, to enhance the clarity and drama of the ballet.

Preparing the performance area at the Royal Academy of Dancing College (PHOTO: *Cristina Aguiar)*

Cueing with or without a score

A dance performance may not have an actual score, so you might wonder if Stage Managers need to be able to read music. For opera and musicals, the answer will be yes, and an assistant stage manager will be employed by English National Ballet only if he or she can read music or is prepared to learn.

Cues can be taken aurally, rather than visually following the score's notation, so the Stage Manager will hear the high note which signifies a cue, rather than seeing the black dots on the page.

Visual cues

However, when it comes to dance, other visual skills are necessary. Whereas *Swan Lake* has a traditional score, many pieces have music or sound accompaniment which does not have traditional musical notation, therefore the 'score' signifies something different. Rather than relying solely on musical bars, the stage manager needs to become familiar with 'landmarks' of sound, and must develop a high level of skill in movement observation, to take visual cues from the dancers' movements.

A typical visual cue Suppose a lighting effect is to be produced as a group of dancers raise their arms in unison. The lighting designer will decide at which point in the action the light is to reach the required strength, and the Stage Manager must give the cue to the operator at the precise moment which will result in synchronisation. If this arm movement has accompaniment with a regular beat, it will be able to be 'counted out', and will happen at the same time each performance. If, however, the sound has a freer relationship with the choreography, and the two are not intended to occur 'in sync.', the Stage Manager will decide whether to take a visual or aural cue. The light cue is likely to coincide with the movement rather than the sound, so a visual cue is needed, and it is the Stage Manager's powers of observation and feeling for the speed and dynamic of the dancers' performance, a kinaesthetic sense, that will determine the sensitivity and accuracy of the resulting effect.

Cueing the lighting board operators

The Stage Manager must cue the operators ahead of time, allowing for the seconds needed for speaking and the time for the technician to execute the instruction. The cues will generally be plotted into a computer, each one having a precise duration, so once the button is pressed, they will occur identically at each performance. In a theatre, the Stage Manager delivers the cues from the prompt corner, through headphones (cans) to the board operators.

Annie Lincoln advises those cueing dance for the first time, 'The style of delivery of cues is as important as the timing. The operators need succinct and consistent instructions from the Stage Manager in order to press the buttons at exactly the right time. Too many words can be confusing, and instructions like "Anticipate the entrance of the soloist" or "Go just before the third *arabesque*" usually result in an inaccurate cue. After the traditional "Stand by" instruction, I prefer to make the word "Go!" the point at which the button is pressed, preceding this by "LX cue so and so" followed by a slight pause. The pause ensures the operators are ready. "Go!" is the magic word and should always be uttered last in each group of instructions.'

On tour, the operators may belong to the venue, and occasionally are inexperienced. She tells a hilarious 'horror story' where the theatre's relay system to the dressing rooms and the headset cueing system had been cross-wired, When problems inevitably arose as various lighting changes did not happen, or were late, Annie was told by the operator, 'Well this is a 24-way board, and I've only got ten fingers, see, so I've been using a pencil across some of the switches. The problem is that I keep dropping my pencil.' Because of the cross-wiring, the dancers in the dressing room were highly amused to be also privy to this conversation!

Annie also emphasises the value of score reading over taking visual cues, 'During one performance of *Swan Lake*, the dancer performing Prince Siegfried was making his début, and forgot to make his "vow swearing" movement at the appointed time, despite frantic prompting from the other dancers. This action was accompanied by an important lighting change, and was marked on the score.' Her ability to take the cue from the score meant that the lighting stayed on course, even if the drama lapsed momentarily.

Contemporary choreographers often challenge the accepted ways of cueing. Movement material may be created with the dancers in rehearsal, but only finalised a couple of days before the opening performance. Experimental choreography means that there is no traditional terminology to identify the movements against which cues are plotted and, in addition, these can only be recognised at the very last minute, requiring a cool head and acute powers of observation from the Stage Manager!

Informal situations still require the show to be run and cued professionally, but the set-up can only be decided once in the actual performance space. Annie Lincoln says that on ENB's small-scale tours, concert halls and other non-theatre venues may

CHECK: OPENING LIGHT
    CHANDELIER IN
    GAUZE IN
    SATIN IN
    TABS IN
    IRON OUT
    DSOP WL LIGHT
12 COURT COUPLES
    BLUEBIRDS
    PRINCE
    AURORA

S/B. HOUSELIGHTS OUT
    CONDUCTOR'S LIGHT
    TAB DRESSING OUT
    LX Q's 93 94 95
    FLY Q's 1, 2, 3
    DSOP

ON CLEARANCE. - CONDUCTOR S/B
   THEN HOUSELIGHTS OUT
    CONDUCTOR INTO PIT -
    COND'S LIGHT UP + DOWN
  WHEN SET - TAB DRESSING OUT

ON 1st NOTE:-
        FLYS Q1 GO-TABS
  WHEN ¾ OUT LX Q 93 GO
  5s

  5s   LX Q 94) GO
SATIN ↑¾ FLY Q 2)
  DEAD

         LX Q95) GO
SATIN OUT FLY Q 3)
CHAND. TO FLY DEAD
GAUZE OUT DSOP)

CALL: CURTAIN UP
    ON ACT III.

Annie Lincoln's cue sheets for The Sleeping Beauty

SWANSONG STAGE MANAGEMENT CUEING SHEET	ENGLISH NATIONAL BALLET	PAGE 1/3
CHECK: 3 BEGINNERS.		
2 CANES IN M.S.O.P. BAY		
CIGARETTE AND LIGHTER WITH 1 MAN		
NOSE WITH 1st INTERROGATOR		
2 HATS WITH INTERROGATORS		
CHAIR IN U.S. POSITION O.P.		
OPENING LIGHT: POOL ROUND CHAIR.		
SMOKE MACHINE HOT		
S/B HOUSE LIGHTS OUT		
TAB DRESSING OUT		
LX Q1	VICTIM SITTING ON CHAIR O.P.	
TABS OUT		
ON CLEARENCE WHEN READY:	SMOKE GO TO HANG IN AIR - THEN	
	TABS GO	
	then when out -	
	LX Q 1 GO	7 secs
2 INTERROGATORS ENTER M.S.O.P. THEY TAP DANCE D.S.O.P. OF CHAIR. THEY GO 1 EACH SIDE OF VICTIM.		
AS THEY START 'INTERROGATING' TAP EACH SIDE:		
S/B SOUND Q 1	S.R. INTERROGATOR TAPS	
LX Q 1a	S.L. INTERROGATOR TAPS	
AS 1st INTERROGATOR RAISES ARM TO STRIKE	S.R. INTERROGATOR TAPS:	
VICTIM'S HEAD: ⟶	SOUND Q 1 ⎫ GO	3 secs.
	LX Q 1a ⎭	
CALL CURTAIN UP		
2nd CRASH -		
S/B LX Q 2: 1 INTEROGGATOR EACH SIDE OF MAN COLLAPSED IN CHAIR.		
ON INTRO TO 1st TAP(REGULAR PERCUSSIVE BEATS START:'THE 8's): ⟶	LX Q2 GO	20 secs
VICTIM DOES SOLO, 2 MEN S.R.		
ON RETURN OF TUNE:		
S/B LX Q 3:		
AS MAN SITS ON LAST NOTE OF TUNE: ⟶	LX Q 3 GO	↑ 2secs↓4 secs
AS SILENT INTERROGATION STARTS: -		
S/B LX Q 4		
SOUND Q 2		
INTERROGATORS PUT ON NOSE AND HATS.		
THEY START TO WALK UPSTAGE OF CHAIR: ⟶	LX Q 4 GO	5 secs
THEY TOUCH CAPS AND TURN TO FACE C.S.		
AS THEY LIFT FOOT FOR 1st STEP: ⟶	SOUND Q 2 GO - 'TEA FOR TWO'	
AS VICTIM JOINS IN (ALL 3 D.S.O.P.):		
S/B LX Q 5;		
ALL SLIDE TO U.S.P.S.		
AS THEY START TO WALK ACROSS BACK IN LINE:⟶	LX Q 5 GO (1st beat of phrase) 5 secs	
	continued....	

Annie Lincoln's cue sheet for Swansong

have no prompt corner from which to deliver the cues, commenting, 'You set up a prompt corner wherever it makes sense – it can be as little as a stool, a music stand, a set of cans and a torch. One of the most impromptu ones involved my lying on the floor and peering round the black masking leg. This was the only way to see the stage without being visible to the audience!'

The Royal Academy of Dancing College Workshop studio performance has all technical elements positioned behind the backcloth, with wings created by tying black legs onto girders in the studio's ceiling. The sound system, containing reel-to-reel, DAT machine and cassette deck, is situated at one end, with the dimmer racks and lighting board at the opposite end, next to the appropriate power source. The Stage Manager stands next to the lighting board operators and signals the cues to them and sound operators by means of her 'cueing stick'; this is a 6-inch piece of wood (cut off the end of an old ballet *barre*) which is covered with luminous tape. this is visible, even in the dark, to the technicians and dancers, and the Stage Manager's various gestures communicate instructions, such as 'Music – GO!' or 'Dancers onstage – GO!'.

Whatever your set-up, take time to work out and practise cueing systems. Flexibility is the key factor. Compare cue sheets for English National Ballet's *Swan Lake* and *Swansong*.

11. Administration, Funding, Publicity and Marketing

Dance administration can be a tough job, especially if it involves a new company struggling to get established. Administrators frequently do their job single-handed, if they cannot afford assistants, and need as much encouragement as the artists. As well as battling with small budgets, they must find and book the performance and rehearsal venues, plan the travel, apply for funding, hook the sponsors, do the marketing, publicity, timetables, book the collaborators, find money to pay everyone ... and so on. This is in addition to answering the phone, writing letters, paying the bills, making the tea, soothing the artists...

It is not a job for the faint-hearted, and any innocent youngster considering that a career in 'dance admin.' is an easy way to earn a buck should stop right here!

Support for dance administrators

Dance UK runs the Management Liaison Group, a regular talking shop for administrators of small and middle-scale dance companies. Dance UK 'supports and raises the profile of dance in the United Kingdom. As an independent, non-profit-making organisation for all forms of professional dance, it voices the needs of the profession including individual dance artists, companies, choreographers, administrators and technicians.

FUNDING

The money for a dance production comes basically from three sources:

- a grant or other award
- sponsorship
- fund-raising events.

Grants

Established companies will be in receipt of funding from several sources, including sponsorship, plus revenue finding (from national or regional arts bodies) or a project grant. Revenue funding provides an annual amount of money and a project grant funds an individual venture. Grants may be applied for from the Arts Council of England, the Scottish Arts Council or Regional Arts Associations. The introduction of National Lottery money has affected funding for all the arts, including dance.

Grants from arts associations are generally awarded only after proof of worth, so it is likely that most recipients will have started out without this type of funding and earned their spurs over a number of years.

Production costs may also be found through fund-raising events and sponsorship, with revenue from ticket sales offsetting those costs after the event. So you need to have sufficient funds to get the show on the road or, at least, into the theatre.

Sponsorship

The lists of sponsors in dance companies' programmes will give you an idea of larger organisations with an interest in helping the arts, and it is worth remembering that in Britain, ABSA, the Association of Business Sponsorship for the Arts, exists to foster this kind of connection, making an annual award to the firm considered to have given the best support in that year. Whilst ABSA is primarily an organisation which deals with the business sponsor, rather than the production needing the money, they run a Pairing Scheme on behalf of the Department of National Heritage, whereby they will match any business offer to an arts project, thus doubling the amount available.

Do not be diffident in approaching businesses for assistance – you have nothing to lose. Sponsorship plans must be set in motion far in advance of the production period – at least a year ahead. Even the best laid plans can suffer a hiccup, so the fund-raising schedule should be properly thought through.

Sponsorship can be modest Sponsorship does not necessarily mean the offer of vast sums. Retailers with a vested interest, like the ballet shoe makers and dance flooring specialists, often help, and all assistance should be acknowledged in the programme plus an offer of complimentary tickets.

Local business Local businesses should be contacted, as recognition of their help in the programme is good publicity, and press coverage of the performance ensures the sponsor's name gets further exposure. Assistance can also come in kind, larger stores offering vouchers for raffling, and dancewear firms donating garments for prizes or costumes.

Fund-raising events

These can range from cake and jumble sales, parties and discos, to competitions, raffles and small-scale sponsored events, such as swims and walks. At the performances, you can sell programmes, posters, photographs, T-shirts with the group's name, plus drinks and nibbles.

Modest events like these are only scaled-down versions of the huge galas and balls which are held to raise funds for larger ventures.

Funds can be raised for professional or student projects. The Royal Academy of Dancing College students raise their own funds to cover production costs. Money is raised by Christmas for March performances, and during the previous Summer term, each student writes ten letters to possible sponsors. Local shops, businesses, restaurants, banks and building societies are approached, plus specialist dance shops. Addresses are found via Yellow Pages, local papers and dance magazines. Fund-raising events range from contests like 'guess-the-number-of-sweets-in-a-jar', to car washing, carol singing and non-uniform days.

Fund raising can be arduous, and it helps to involve friends and relatives for encouragement. You might find a friend with a business who is willing to support your venture. Woody Allen's film *Bullets Over Broadway* satirises the whole business of backing a show and depicts the hilarious and terrifying result of friends' involvement. It is a real tonic to weary fund raisers, and should be watched on video when the going gets tough!

Where to find advice

The Place Dance Services, one of the National Dance Agencies, offers its members many services, including advice on funding. They will advise on the selection of charitable trusts and foundations appropriate to a particular project, and the nitty-gritty of making an application. Dance UK also offers its members an information sheet on Trusts and Funds.

Key publications on arts funding include *The Arts Funding Guide* from the Directory of Social Change, *The Hollis Arts Funding Handbook, European Guide to Foundations and Sponsors* and *Courrier d'Europe*. Addresses at the end of the book.

PUBLICITY AND MARKETING

The importance of matching company and venue has already been mentioned, with the need to assess, target and build an audience. Good marketing and publicity ensure that a company will have the highest possible exposure and profile, with education work being a major tool.

Publicity consists of getting a company's name and work known to as wide an audience as possible, with the aim of attracting them to the show. People today are bombarded with information and advertisements in the media, so an image should be found which accurately evokes the work, and has sufficient impact to stick in the public mind.

Finding your identity

Identify what your group does, how if differs from other dance groups and why people should come to the show. In other words, what are you selling them? Why should they come to see your work?

An information pack, however modest, is essential. It can be sent out to the press, theatre managers, funding bodies and anyone else who might be interested. It should comprise:

- the general aim of the group
- details of performances
- details and biographies of director, choreographer, composer, designer
- details and biographies of the dancers
- details of sponsors
- press cuttings
- photographs, if you have any.

A popular programme

If you are building an audience, consider what will make them come to the show. If you have music which will appeal to a particular audience, or guest musicians, or a

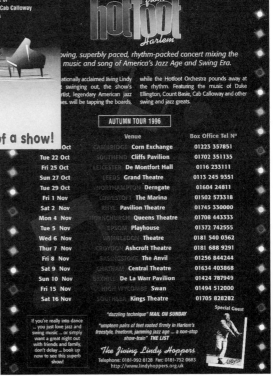

Leaflet produced by the Jiving Lindy Hoppers for one of their productions

local designer, or local *anything*, capitalise on it, and feature it in your advertising. Programme planning is about targeting an audience, as well as creating a balanced programme. Christopher Bruce's *Rooster*, to The Rolling Stones' music was a smash hit for London Contemporary Dance Theatre and Rambert Dance Company. Its inclusion in a programme brought people to the show, introducing them to other works in the process.

A ballet company will be expected to deliver the well-known classical ballets. *The Nutcracker* is a sure-fire winner at Christmas, introducing many children to their first ballet, and the classics may be so popular that theatre managers may demand a ballet company performs only these, in preference to triple bills or more adventurous work which may not fill the seats.

Offer a package

Open classes, workshops and talks are an excellent back-up to a performance. You could offer these to local schools and arts groups, inexpensively, combining the cost of both performance and workshop. As well as whetting your audience's appetite, education work can also help build a group's identity and clarify and develop its unique characteristics.

The companies featured in the second part of this book have developed distinct identities and artistic policies. The publicity strategies often include extensive education work. To give you an idea of how these aspects work in practice, I have included examples from their information packs, with examples of both publicity and education-oriented leaflets, and extracts from their artistic policy or mission-statements.

Planning your campaign

Schedule what you are going to do over the number of weeks available. Identify appropriate media sources and make contact. Find out who to write to and the deadlines. These may include:

- local press – newspapers, magazines
- national press
- local radio and TV
- specialist press, like *The Dancing Times*

You will need to print leaflets and posters, and decide where they will be sent or placed. Programmes can be printed later in the process, and can include advertising which will bring in extra revenue, so target anyone you can think of and offer inexpensive advertising space.

Publicity by the venue

The venue also has a responsibility towards promotion and publicity, and a close relationship should be built up between organisers at both ends, each being kept fully informed of what the other is doing, and all parties fully aware of each other's expectations.

School or college shows

Publicity for a school or college show can draw on the help of the umbrella organisation.

12. Rehearsals and Production Week __

THE STUDIO

The rehearsal period is when the creative process happens, and a happy and productive time is the best preparation for the theatre. The studio's facilities make a major contribution to the working atmosphere, so find the best hall you can afford. Important considerations are:

The dimensions Basic dimensions for a dance studio start from a minimum of 8.6m × 6.1m (25ft × 20ft). A small-scale company will need 12m × 13m (40ft × 43ft), rising to 18m × 19m (60ft × 63ft) for a large group. Headroom should be a minimum of 4.0m (13ft 2in) to a maximum of 6.0m (19ft 8in) – remember men jumping and lifts! If the studio is large enough, the dimensions of the eventual performance area, complete with wings, should be marked out on the floor with tape.

Flooring See chapter 2

Heating and ventilation These are of the utmost importance to dancers. Cold conditions are injurious to the muscles, and may be dangerous. The actors' (and dancers') union, Equity, lays down a minimum temperature of 65 degrees. As well as allowing fresh air, ventilation also includes air-conditioning, or fans, in hot weather, and the absence of draughts in winter.

Electrical points and their location You will need a convenient spot to plug in your rehearsal sound system or portable tape recorder, somewhere where you can see the dancers clearly. This excludes a point out in the hall, unless you have an extension lead, high up on the wall, or hidden behind piles of furniture.

Piano (if needed) This is an important consideration for some groups. If not already on site, it can be difficult, or impossible, to bring in a piano.

Changing rooms and showers Whilst most dancers will tolerate basic facilities, there should be a minimum standard of space available, with sufficient heating, privacy and security. Washing or, ideally, showering facilities should be available.

Refreshment facilities If the studio does not have a kitchen, you will need to take in an electric kettle and supplies for short breaks. You may be lucky enough to have refreshment facilities on site but, if not, consider if there is anywhere to eat close by. Dancers cannot nip out as easily as office workers, as they have to change clothing and possibly shower, so a long trek to the nearest café will not be popular.

General location A warm studio on a bitter winter's day, with a non-slip, resilient floor, hot water and proximity to shops and 'civilisation' seems a simple demand, but not always easy to find. A central location will add to the dancers' sense of well-being and allow somewhere to escape to in the break. A centrally situated church hall might be preferable to a more glamorous venue miles from anywhere.

Where to find a studio

Large towns and cities usually have dance studios. They may house a vocational school or a private teacher, and there are also complexes devoted exclusively to classes in different dance disciplines on an 'open' basis. Studios like these should be well equipped, meaning a decent floor, *barres*, mirrors and even a piano.

Church halls Good dance studios are not always cheap, but there are alternatives. One may hear of a children's ballet school 'in a church hall down the road'. A resident children's dance school will probably hold classes after school hours, which means that the hall may be free earlier in the day. There may be a reasonable wood or lino floor, and possibly a piano. Such halls are unlikely to have showers, but there is often a kitchen where you can make a hot drink.

Everything but a decent floor A studio with everything except a non-slip floor could be transformed by a portable linoleum, and if you are there for a substantial period, suggest laying the floor for the duration. If barres are a necessity, invest in portable ones and transport them in.

THE REHEARSAL SCHEDULE

A realistic, well-structured rehearsal schedule is a synthesis of the needs of all the different parties involved, allowing each one the time and conditions necessary to bring work to fruition. No artist ever feels he has sufficient time and rarely believes that his work is ready for the first theatre call but, as Francis Reid asserts, 'In theatre, there is no such thing as late delivery of the finished product. The customers (audience) have contracts (tickets) and, at the appointed hour on the appointed day, they come to collect the product (performance) in person'.

A good director will encourage communication amongst collaborators, and between departments if they exist, and the schedule should be agreed by all participants.

Artistic planning

As well as the logistics of getting everyone together, the choreographer or director also has to consider the artistic development which happens during the rehearsal period. He must pace the rehearsal plan, so that each element reaches the right pitch of performance before the first stage rehearsal. Everything, and everyone, must be ready, but must not 'peak too soon'.

With a revival this may be easy to gauge, but a new creation has more unknown factors.

Each part of the production needs sufficient preparation. Rehearsals with a large group may take longer than those involving soloists or a small cast. So make sure you have allowed enough time. You may find that you do not practise the beginning of the work at the beginning of the rehearsal period; the dancers' availability or your own preference might mean that you start with a sequence from the middle of the piece, or even the end!

Plan to do something relatively easy at the beginning of rehearsals. Leave possibly sticky bits until the middle of the rehearsal period. Don't leave them until the end or you'll panic!

It encourages the dancers to have something to get their teeth into and practise, so you might start off with a 'dancy' bit and inspiring music. Something which moves, but isn't too technically demanding. If you are working with partners who have not worked together before, don't rush in with something impossibly difficult which makes each dancer feel insecure in the presence of the other. Work in gently and with sensitivity. Even if you are quaking in your boots, give your dancers confidence. Don't expect too much too soon. Artistic development grows as a flower unfolds; don't wrench it up from its roots before it is ready, just to satisfy your impatience. It doesn't work.

Explaining what is to happen in the theatre

If you are working with young people, and others unused to being in a theatre, it is important to talk to them about what is to happen once they are in the performance venue. It is good to do this towards the end of the studio rehearsal period. Its timing should be considered; if you suspect that there will be a day where everyone is tired and crabby, it can transform the atmosphere to remind the dancers how worthwhile all their hard work has been and how exciting it will be 'on the night'. Ensure that they are familiar with theatre terms and conventions, outlined in chapter 1.

PRODUCTION WEEK

Transferring a work from studio to theatre occurs in the run-up to a first performance, or as part of a tour with various dates and venues. Production week denotes the period prior to and including the first performance, in which the get-in, fit-up, technical and dress-rehearsals take place. However, many companies do not have the week that the term suggests; in fact, on tour, there may be just a single day or only a few hours in which to set up and 'place' a show. Those who give morning matinées in schools will simply set up, warm up and go on!

Whether there are three hours or three days before the show, certain procedures are common to most productions. If a new work or revival is to open a season, it will generally occur after a substantial rehearsal period, with all collaborators coming together at the end. During the final days of studio rehearsals, the composer, and possibly musicians, will have been present, and the designer and wardrobe team will have been on hand to supervise fittings. The dancers will try out costumes by actually dancing in them. Lighting designer and technician will have been monitoring the almost-finished work. At the venue, administrative and technical details will be finalised, ensuring everything is ready for the company's get-in, including the get-out of the previous production, often during the night before. Publicity and marketing arrangements should have ensured that bookings are well under way.

The get-in

The technical and administrative staff often arrive at the venue ahead of the dancer, to start work on backstage and onstage facilities. The technical staff will unload sets and lighting equipment, and the wardrobe team may possibly arrive with costumes.

It stands to reason that the venue will have been notified of exactly when a group is to arrive. Make sure that caretakers, if it is a school or college, have been kept fully informed, or you may turn up to find that everywhere is locked and there is no-one to let you in! Or the heating is turned off and it is in the middle of winter. Or there are people using the rooms you need.

You should know, by name, who to liaise with on arrival, especially if the venue's staff work in shifts. Bill, whom you spoke to on the phone, may be working another shift, and you have to deal with Fred, who has never heard of you! This may sound far-fetched, but you would be amazed how lines can get crossed and mis-understandings arise.

If there are only you and the dancers, you will need to remember to take such essential items as:

- iron
- sewing kit, including safety pins
- spare tights, leotards, shoes
- rosin
- first aid supplies
- marking tape and Sellotape
- spare make-up
- towels
- sweets
- something to drink – say, water or fruit juice. Hopefully you won't need anything stronger!

Lighting (see also chapter 9)

Rigging and focusing After the get-in, the technical crew will rig the lights. This process involves hanging and cabling lights according to the lighting designer's plan, copies of which will have been distributed to the technicians. Scenic elements such as cloths, gauzes and free-standing sets will be put into place, then the lights will be focused. Focusing is a crucial part of the lighting process, controlling the exact angle at which each light beam hits the person or object to be lit. Inaccuracies can destroy an effect. When time is limited and a soft edge is required from all sidelights, a way of avoiding the time-consuming adjustment of lenses is to focus them with a hard edge, then drop a piece of 'frost', a kind of gel, into the colour frame. This diffuses the beam and gives a soft edge.

Rigging and focusing are lengthy procedures, and the greater number of lights, the longer it takes. Always ensure you have enough time for all the lighting aspects.

Plotting With the lights focused and the scenery in place, the lighting designer will begin to plot the lighting states, working with the Stage Manager and technicians who operate the lighting board. Dancers or stand-ins will be onstage in costume. This will be the first time that all visual elements of the production are seen *in situ*, and the lighting designer may adjust his plan to accommodate any differences which become apparent: colours and textures in the set and costumes may look slightly different from anticipated, and certain spacing elements may change with the transfer from studio to performing area. The lighting cues will be plotted in order and entered on computer, although situations may demand that some or all of the cues are operated manually.

Cueing the beginning of a show At the beginning of a show, there needs to be a cueing system from the front of house to the stage area, letting the performers and stage crew know that the audience is seated and the performance can begin. From this point on, everything is in the hands of the Stage Manager.

In a venue without tabs or curtains, and with a revealed stage, whilst the audience is entering, it is likely that there will be a pre-set. This is a simple pre-performance lighting state which subtly highlights the stage area and helps create an atmosphere of anticipation. In this case the pre-set will be the first lighting state to be plotted, and on the day of the show, it will be put up before the audience enters and will remain on until the cue to fade it out at the start of the performance. The following cue is likely to be 'Houselights – GO!'

From then on, the lighting designer will build each state, experimenting then finalising the details. If the actual dancers are present, it can be helpful for them to 'walk' through certain sequences, so that their precise placement onstage can be clarified and the exact timing of visual cues monitored. However, a lighting rehearsal is not 'dancers' time', and should not be used as a movement rehearsal, although it can be used to get a feel of the space and a sense of where the lights are. 'Finding the light' is the process of feeling when you are in the right spot to be effectively lit, and not just outside it, or in a 'dark' space such as an unlit apron at the front of the stage.

Lighting rehearsals can take considerable time, and much patience may be needed, but it is an exciting period, when at last the production starts to have a finished look to it. Good lighting is not dependent on a large number of states so much as the effectiveness of each one and its contribution to the whole.

Stage and dress rehearsals

One or more full dress rehearsals will take place after the lighting has been plotted and all other aspects of stage preparation are completed. The time available for stage rehearsals varies enormously, but by and large no company ever feels that their work is ready for the first performance, however many stage calls they have had.

Running through prior to the dress rehearsal If there is time, it is preferable for the dancers to run through a dance onstage, perhaps with live music and some costumes, before the official dress rehearsal. The first time onstage is exciting but stressful, and it helps performers to cope with unknown factors if they do not face all of them at once. The dimensions of the stage, entrances and exits, 'finding the light', live music and quick changes are all new considerations. Whilst the dancers are getting accustomed to them, the technical and emotional levels of the performance may decline in intensity, to build again once all the staging aspects have been absorbed and become familiar.

In less formal situations, technical staff can often use the dancers' try-out sessions onstage to recap cueing points. The musicians can practise working together and taped music can be tested for sound levels. In a theatre, this time and freedom to fine-tune and co-ordinate does not always exist, and sometimes everything comes together only at the dress rehearsal.

Dress rehearsals Dress rehearsals are nerve-wracking events for all those concerned, not just the dancers, and a good director or choreographer will keep the whole production flowing as smoothly as possible and soothe any ruffled feathers. It is generally better to keep the performance moving, and only stop if something goes seriously wrong. All the participants will have sticky patches and these are better discussed and sorted out at the end. The aim is to ensure that no one element dominates and holds up the proceedings for the others.

To co-ordinate all the staging elements and personnel is a mammoth and very skilled task.

RESTAGING

Take care if you are restaging a work. In the professional world, strict copyright laws may apply to the works of an established choreographer and, on his death, a trust may be set up to grant permission for a company to stage a work and to oversee its production.

Choreographers are notoriously particular about how a work is performed and by whom, and not all groups who wish to mount a piece will be given permission. Established repertory dance companies go to great lengths to acquire specific works which will enhance their programmes and challenge their dancers, and an exciting acquisition will stimulate interest and draw audiences.

Whether a piece is by an international choreographer or an aspirant, the person in charge of teaching the work and overseeing all the production aspects will generally be chosen by the creator or the trust. It may be a key dancer who worked closely with the choreographer, a choreologist who notated the work, or the ballet master or mistress who rehearsed it. In all cases the main concern is that the choreographer's intentions is faithfully reproduced. The intimacy of the choreographer/dancer relationship means that the movement is a result of both parties' work, and when you consider the influence of the original dancers, it is easy to see how a 'second-hand' version can result in something different.

In the case of designs, they are either recreated according to the original by the designer (who owns the copyright) or, after the designer's death, recreated 'in the style of' the original. Or a new designer might be found to redesign the work from scratch.

13. Health and Safety, Sanity and Therapy

THE VENUE

All venues holding performances are subject to health and safety rules and regulations. They will be regularly checked for fire risks, and you must make sure that anything you take in will not breach the rules. Discuss what you will be bringing in with the manager of your venue as soon as your booking is finalised.

Apart from the general legal requirements, there are extra health and safety concerns which apply to venues for dance. Flooring has already been discussed. Heating is another prime consideration. Cold conditions are dangerous for dancers: remember the minimum temperature (20°C/65°F) for working conditions. Ventilation is also important, and there should be adequate washing and showering facilities. There should be no problem in a full-time theatre, but in a non-theatre space, you may have to remind the staff to put the heating and hot water on, particularly if the building has not been in use during the days prior to your arrival. So check, and double-check! If you think it prudent, take with you the largest blow-heater you can easily carry, along with an electric kettle and extension lead.

KEEPING GOING

Dance producers endure periods of great creative energy alternating with spells of exhaustion and aridity. The latter are exacerbated by practical problems as well as artistic doubts. The strain of finding funds, organising rehearsals and keeping up the morale of dancers, musicians and designers can be very draining. So how can you keep going?

Body and mind

Look after two areas – the body and the mind.

Greater awareness exists today of the anatomical needs of dancers, and there has been much research into how to maintain the dancer's body in optimum physical condition. Dance teachers undergo rigorous training to ensure a sound understanding of anatomy, essential when they are entrusted with the development of children's bodies and minds, and must prepare students to meet the intense demands made on today's professional dancers. Those in authority are now rightly expected to show concern for the welfare of dancers in their charge. So you must look after your dancers.

Injuries prevail which were much less common thirty years ago: stress fractures, for example, are now commonplace. Specialist centres have been set up like the Dancers' Remedial Clinic in London, and the findings of sports medicine specialists are being increasingly applied to dance. Pilates training is becoming increasingly popular to help maintain fitness and correct technique. *Dance Technique and Injury Prevention* and Dance UK's *Fit to Dance?* should be read by all those in charge of dancers. Dance UK also offer a Medical Register Helpline for dancers.

Avoiding injury and maintaining fitness Warming up and warming down before and after class or rehearsal, has an enormous effect on the prevention of injuries; you must ensure that you give your dancers the time for this.

Major companies and schools have physiotherapy departments. Complementary therapies are also popular, including homeopathy, acupuncture, osteopathy and chiropractic. Personal recommendation within the close-knit dance world usually ensure that most dancers find the help they need.

Long-term health in female dancers has been highlighted by publicity concerning osteoporosis, research showing a connection between the condition and bodyweight. This concerns everyone working with female dancers, especially between the ages of twelve and twenty. The emphasis on an aesthetically pleasing body and the preoccupation with being slim exert huge pressure on developing teenagers; every effort must be made to ensure they eat a healthy diet.

Young dancers must take care, not only of their diet but also of their energy expenditure. Some get so 'wound up' that they feel unable to stop and rest – believing if they take a day off, their technique will suffer. Competition and high standards cause dancers to be over- rather than under-conscientious, and adequate rest must be taken.

Emphasis should also be laid on the inner world of the dancer, on mental and emotional well-being. Considerable stresses are endured by performing artists and choreographers; even a measure of success brings pressure to maintain standards and to progress. The anxiety of competition for roles in dancers on long-term contracts, and the demands of finding the next job for freelancers, push many into abandoning their careers early.

PART TWO

PROFESSIONAL DANCE COMPANIES

The Jiving Lindy Hoppers

The Jiving Lindy Hoppers are regarded as Britain's most accessible and exciting authentic jazz dance company. Founded in 1984, with their first performance at the Notting Hill Carnival, they have toured extensively throughout the UK, USA and Japan, winning awards for both performances and pioneering work in education – including a 1991 Sainsbury's Arts Education Award, a Digital Dance Award, a Barclays New Stages Award and a Gulbenkian Foundation Dance Award.

Terry Monaghan, co-founder and now Research and Development Director of the company is committed to the establishment and recognition of authentic jazz dance as an art form both popular and serious in its own right. Inspired by Whitey's Lindy Hoppers, the black American company highly successful in the 1930s at New York's Savoy Ballroom, Monaghan's achievement has been remarkable and a fine example of passion, single-mindedness and shrewd common sense. Monaghan teamed up with dancer and teacher Warren Heyes in 1983, after meeting at the rock and roll society at the University of London Union. Amazed by the lack of representation of authentic jazz dance in the professional dance world, and the apparent neglect of a tradition with immense popularity, Monaghan and Heyes began giving public classes, leading to the Jiving Lindy Hoppers' first performance. Since then, their dates have ranged from theatre, concert and cabaret gigs, schools' residencies and TV and film appearances in Britain, to the Lincoln Center in New York!

This diversity calls for tremendous flexibility and professionalism. The Jiving Lindy Hoppers perform with a variety of bands, ranging from a duo of piano and percussion to a full jazz orchestra, these performances being instigated by either the JLH or the bands themselves, the latter often calling upon the dancers to take part in what is primarily a music gig.

A key feature of the company's uniqueness is the presentation and preservation of social dance forms in a performance setting – the Charleston, Black Bottom, Lindy Hop, Rock and Roll – are the basis of dances choreographed with meticulous attention to detail and authenticity, which have the advantage of being immediately accessible to the audience by their familiarity. Everyone feels they 'know' the Charleston or Jive. As Monaghan says, 'The Lindy, like Tap, was one of the few street dances that eventually reached performance level via the world of social dance. It was the dance counterpoint to Swing music and they evolved together. The flowing phrases and the orchestrated big band sound created the music for a dance form whose varying sequences could match the band's arrangements. In turn the frenetic couples drove the soloists on to wilder degrees of improvisation. The starting point was the smoothing out of the snappy two step sequences of the Charleston. The competitive couples absorbed the repertoire of American vernacular dance and insatiably searched through everything from classical ballet to judo to find "original" steps.'*

The JLH programmes began small. 'It was more like an act in the early days, drawing on a series of individual short dances,' says Monaghan, who has played many roles in the company's history, at various points devising the shows, dancing, managing, driving the van and acting as technician. As the company has grown in reputation and popularity, several full-length productions have been created, and they have gradually been able to expand to having a full-time Company Director, Eileen Feeney, and Artistic Director, Carolene Hinds. Technically, resources have meant that they have been reliant on facilities provided by individual venues, with the exception of the full-length *Jungle of the Cities*, created in 1994, which enjoyed the luxury of having a lighting designer and technician exclusively for the production.

This was possible through funding from three sources – a substantial project grant from the Arts Council, a Barclays New Stages Award and a commission from Southern Arts which sparked off the idea. Southern Arts needed a new dance production to celebrate the redevelopment of the Corn Exchange, Newbury, as an Arts Centre, aiming to draw audiences not only to the opening performance, but also to the Centre subsequently, and the Jiving Lindy Hoppers' style, appealing right across ages, sexes and cultures, was ideal. The whole package involved a month-long run of performances, education and community work, and, for the first time, the company could afford a properly designed set, in this case a wrestling ring, and a lighting designer.

When subsequently taken on a tour round England, they were able to employ a relighting designer/technical manager, who relit the piece for each date, liaising in advance with each venue and going ahead of the company to hang the specials and refocus the rig. She also hired in any extra equipment as needed. Eileen Feeney said, 'This was a real luxury. Philippa Wickham, had her own transport and simply got on with the job. The band featured in the show was also self-sufficient, allowing Artistic Director, Carolene Hinds, to concentrate on the artistic direction of the production and the dancers.'

However ideal this experience was, Terry and Eileen emphasise that this is not the norm. 'Our flexibility is a blessing, but it also means occasional inconsistencies in the staging aspect of our shows,' they say, 'and unless people fully understand that our commitment to being accessible to all, means that we may often perform in extremely limited conditions, then our very willingness to take dance to new places can mean we are unfairly judged.' Just how much compromise they are prepared to make is sometimes problematic.

Another major presentation, *Echoes of Harlem*, culminated in four performances at London's Royal Court Theatre, a venue not generally associated with dance. 'The lighting staff at the theatre really went to town on *Echoes of Harlem*', remembers Eileen, 'and the performance looked wonderful. Some weeks later, we were performing in a tent/marquee in Bath, with a different band and singer. Assessors from funding bodies came to the Bath show on the strength of reports on the Royal Court. Unfortunately, the lack of proper technical back up at this venue meant they

*Terry Monaghan, 'The Jiving Lindy Hoppers', *Impulse*. Winter/Spring 1986.

Warren Heyes of the Jiving Lindy Hoppers giving a workshop in Drumchapel, Glasgow (PHOTO: *Brian Slater*)

went away disappointed, and were unable to appreciate that, in fact, the show was the same as that at the Royal Court!'

It is a sad situation if a company appears to be penalised for offering a service totally in line with aims claimed to be at the forefront of funding bodies' policies. Inconsistencies are bound to arise when staging can only be in direct relation to the facilities offered by the venue. It could, perhaps, be argued that venues struggling to meet the needs of dance companies, as well as the companies agreeing to appear in less than perfect conditions, should be helped rather than censured. Paradoxes like this go to underline the determination needed by companies to overcome setbacks.

The Jiving Lindy Hoppers, however, are a thriving company, continually in demand, although they would not wish this fact to lead funding bodies to assume that they would not benefit from financial assistance. Monaghan reflected, 'We have developed a name and reputation without always having the technical resources to

JIVING LINDY HOPPERS - TECHNICAL INFORMATION

TITLE OF SHOW: **ECHOES OF HARLEM**   *(To Taped Music at* ~~Presedet~~ *)*

RUNNING TIME: 1ST HALF: ca. 50
INTERVAL: 20 minutes
2ND HALF ca. 45-50

Please note that the running times are APPROXIMATE. They vary slightly depending upon whether the performance is to live or taped music. The second half ends with audience participation and then a final encore number. However, the total running time including interval does not normally exceed 2 hours.

NO. OF DANCERS: 7 - 8

GET-IN: The company usually aims to arrive by 2pm, to check out performance space warm up, rehearse, run through, liaise with venue technical staff re lighting/sound. Lighting should be rigged up prior to get-in. (In the event of live musical accompaniment, the venue must have set up and tuned piano by this time)

The company must be able to rehearse without interference on the performing area from 2pm. If this presents a problem, this must be discussed with JLH Office immediately on receipt of this techspec and a solution agreed.   Alternative warm-up/rehearsal space must have a suitable floor, be large enough and be WARM.

GET-OUT: 1.5 hours after performance ends.

PARKING: Parking space required for high top LT35 VW Van, reg. E642 HMO
Space for band vehicles if band is booked and JLH management if attending

DRESSING ROOM/S: For dancers: either one each for male/female dancers or one large dressing room. Must be secure and warm with sufficient space for no. of people. If not lockable, lockers or a place where valuables may be placed must be provided.
Hanging Rails, Mirrors including full length, sufficient lighting for making up. Shower facilities. If the company is required to share a dressing room, it must be designated a "No-Smoking" area. Must be close to stage area.

REFRESHMENTS: Tea/Coffee/Soft Drinks & Sandwiches to be provided for dancers during the afternoon. Still water & sufficient glasses must be available offstage during show.

QUICK CHANGE   There are rapid costume changes between each dance number. Unless the dressing rooms are immediately off stage, a quick change area with a hanging rail for the costumes must be provided off stage with enough light for dancers to get changed in. It must be screened or be sufficiently private for girls to change in without being seen by the public or technicians.

PERFORMING AREA: Minimum 20' deep x 30' wide (6m x 9m), wings stage right & left, dancers must be able to enter and exit from each side and get around the back of the stage quickly.

FLOOR: Preferably sprung wooden (not highly polished), level, any gaps
filled, trailing wires safely routed and taped down

If there is a choice between dance lino and wooden floor, the company prefers to dance WITHOUT dance lino.

LIGHTING:	Promoter to provide Lighting barplan no later than 4 weeks before perf and list of lighting equipment. JLH lighting plan attached. Promoter to supply, rig and operatr lighting effects as shown on JLH plan at own expense, including follow spot and operator.
SOUND:	
Taped Music:	Cassette Tape with adequate clear amplification for space. Cued tapes provided. Promoter to provide operator. Foldback/monitors 1 mike on a stand in the wings which can be brought centre stage for vocals

back it up, and we often feel under pressure to deliver in the same way as much better-funded companies.' Revenue from performances goes on payment to the group's members, currently a core group of seven dancers who are supplemented by several part-timers. It is also ploughed back into the company to meet production costs.

Without a permanent technician to handle the lighting, the company has developed a system whereby details of their lighting needs are sent in advance to each venue, who then provide the nearest they can with the facilities available. Technical details for part of *Echoes of Harlem* are reproduced here, and are an excellent example of clear, informative and imaginative instructions.

Green Candle Dance Company

Green Candle Dance Company aims to be 'an effective part of a process of raising dance to a central place in the physical, emotional and intellectual life of society: restoring the birthright of all to communicate, express themselves and enjoy themselves through dance.'* Under the artistic direction of Fergus Early, Green Candle has created vivid, challenging and inventive productions for many different community groups, In its distinctive fusion of choreography, music, text and design, Green Candle produces a complete theatrical experience which energises new audiences.

Founded in 1987 by Fergus Early, the company grew from a recognition of the lack of provision for young audiences identified by the then Greater London Arts. Its first show was created for young children, and since then the company has extended its horizons, recognising the need among many other community groups both to watch and participate in innovative, high quality and accessible performance.*

Such variety of audiences and venues inevitably affects the planning of a new production, and each show is created for and built around the artistic opportunities and practical constraints afforded. In staging terms, the company uniquely exploits all possibilities with imaginative and resourceful results. *The Road Home*, aimed at 11–18 year olds, was created for performance in the traverse form – that is, with the audience on two sides. Fergus Early points out that in a school situation, where the performance may be in a hall, rather than a theatre, without the benefit of raised seating, pupils in the back rows have difficulty seeing the stage. If three rows of seats

*From Green Candle's artistic policy

TECHNICAL QUESTIONNAIRE

Green Candle's performance of *Alanna and the Tree* has some basic technical requirements. We hope the following details will give you a better idea of what we will need and what we will bring with us so that the event can run as smoothly as possible. It would be very useful if you could fill in and return the questionnaire so that we can ensure we are fully prepared. Thank you.

We will bring with us the following equipment:

* CD player   * 8 Lanterns
* Portable cassette deck   * 2 Dimmer racks
* Radio microphone   * Lighting board
* Amplifier

which is sufficient to run the show, however if the performance space is more fully equipped we will add to this with your own equipment.

The performance or stage area needs to be approximately 30'x 30' or 9m x 9m in size at one end of the hall. Please could the floor be swept and cleaned before we arrive. It is important that all the different workspaces should be warm for the beginning of work (approx. 17.5 °C) **which might involve the heating being put on earlier than usual.** We will need 3 tables for our sound and lighting equipment, props and speakers - it will save us valuable time on the day if these could be put in the performance space before we arrive. If school bells are due to ring during the performance we would appreciate it if they could possibly be turned off so that they do not interrupt the show.

It would be very helpful to us if you could send a map with clear directions of where you are situated. (London schools on the large A-Z do not need to do this).

If you have any problems or queries about any of this information please call Green Candle's office on 071 359 8776. Please keep this part of the questionnaire for your own reference.

NAME, ADDRESS & TELEPHONE NO.OF VENUE/SCHOOL AND CONTACT PERSON:

_____

_____

1 Please describe access for a large van (long wheel base) from street to venue/school grounds.

_____

_____

2 Can we unload the van next to the performance space? Please describe.

_____

_____

3 Can we park in the grounds?   YES/NO
   If NO is there parking nearby? Please describe.

_____

_____

Cont\...

4 Will our 4 company members be able to have free or subsidised school dinners?   YES/NO

5 Is it possible to black-out the performance space?

  (please delete as applicable)   NO/PARTIALLY/COMPLETELY

6 How many 13amp power sockets are there in the performance space?

  (please circle) 1 2 3 4 5 more (give number)

7 What lighting and sound equipment do you have that we could use? Please list.

_____

_____

_____

8 Where will the workshop take place?

_____

9 Where will performance take place?

_____

THANK YOU!

PLEASE RETURN TO:

GREEN CANDLE DANCE COMPANY, 309 ABERDEEN HOUSE, 22 HIGHBURY GROVE, LONDON
N5 2DQ. TEL: 0171 359 8776 FAX: 0171 359 5840

---

are placed on two sides, with the performance area in between, a greater number in the audience will be able to see the action. In typically inventive form, Early choreographed the piece around the 'road' which the dancing space represented and which was inherently suggested by the layout of audience and stage, commenting that this form could also work with a 'river' idea. Choreographically, the action progressed down the 'road' and utilised both the practical and symbolic possibilities.

The Road Home was an example of Green Candle's powerful and thought-provoking subject matter, dealing with the plight of displaced persons. It celebrated the stories of four survivors from Cyprus, the Middle East, Ireland and Eastern Europe, using dance, speech, song, sound effects and live music, much of it played by the dancers, to create a stark and moving piece. With the performers speaking, singing and playing instruments as well as dancing, the choreography, music and staging unfolded in a fluid organic way as the stories were told, the survivors

Green Candle Dance Company in Fergus Early's The Road Home *(PHOTO: Hugo Glendinning)*

represented as a close-knit band, mutually supportive and dependent. Elements of folk dance and music were integrated naturally into the dramatic thread, evoking individual cultures, yet curiously universal in application – the music including a haunting violin, penny-whistle, bodhran drum and *a capella* singing in close harmony. Staging aspects included the wheelchair used by one of the dancers who is disabled, which gave rise to a wealth of choreographic images, and a large low trolley, acting in several ways – piled up with the refugees' belongings and dragged along the road, become a platform for musicians and instruments, then depicting a boat at sea. Props included sticks which acted as a sound source, a hunger symbol, tent, prison bars and cross, a crutch which became a gun, and a sheet doubling as a concealing blanket and tablecloth for a Sabbath ritual.

The company's education work is very closely integrated with the performance. 'A workshop and a resource pack are always included as part of a performance package,' says Early, and the resource pack for *The Road Home* shows a serious commitment towards the plight of the dispossessed. Devised with the help of The Minority Rights Group, The Refugee Council and the United Nations High Commission for Refugees, it contains profiles of refugees from many countries. It also contains a leaflet from the Minority Rights Group, 'Integrating Refugee Children into Schools', and ideas for dance, music and drama projects based on the idea of dispossession. A far cry from dance works which could be considered frivolous, presentations like this demonstrate the enormous power of the performing and creative arts for touching people's lives and for bringing about understanding.

Whilst the traverse form worked well for *The Road Home* in secondary schools and colleges, Green Candle prefers fronted shows for primary schools, which require sets no higher than 8ft to suit the low ceilings prevalent in many classrooms. With regard to sets, he favours some kind, wherever possible, 'to transform the space', and these are designed for flexibility of presentation and ease of touring. A curved forest scene is built in sections, some or all of which may be used, depending on the amount of stage space, with the separate sections breaking down into lightweight parts which fit in the company's van.

All music for Green Candle is specially written, much of it by the company's Music and Education Director, Sally Davies, who started her career as a dancer. Designer Craig Givens, another frequent collaborator with Early, also had a dance background. The dancers themselves are required to have singing skills and, if possible, to play an instrument. With speech also an integral part of many presentations, Early comments that occasionally he employs an actress with secondary movement abilities for a production, rather than a dancer who can act.

On tour, Green Candle carries a basic amount of its own equipment, which is able to be easily put up by technician and stage manager, often as early as 8.30 in the morning, in preparation for a show in a school at 10.30 or 11.00 a.m. Their technical equipment consists of 4 × 10–12ft telescopic lighting stands and T-bars, with 2 lanterns per stand plus 2–4 on the floor. Any taped music is recorded onto a CD with a cassette back-up. To give an idea of the requirements for a school or centre, an example of the company's questionnaire is reproduced on pages 114–15.

STAGING DANCE WITH YOUNG PEOPLE

This section looks at several projects involving students and children. These include a 'bridge' between student and professional performance, a project to develop young designers for dance, vocational students dancing a classic, education projects in the state sector and a children's dance school.

Transitions Dance Company

Transitions Dance Company is the result of a unique policy which brings together outstanding international choreographers and skilled young dancers, backed by the expertise of one of Europe's leading institutions for contemporary dance training, the Laban Centre for Movement and Dance, founded in London in 1983 by the eminent American teacher Bonnie Bird, one of the original members of the Martha Graham Company. As Head of Dance Theatre Studies at the Laban Centre, she and Dr Marion North, the Centre's Director, were concerned with bridging the gap between the training years of a potential professional dancer, and his or her establishment as a working artist. The three years of study common in Britain were thought to be insufficient to fulfil a young dancer's potential fully, and it was felt that a further concentrated period would be of value. They, therefore, devised a fourth year of training to take the form of a small performing company, committed not only to developing the skills of its dancers but also, through the Bonnie Bird Choreographic Fund, to the promotion of new, young choreographic talent, whose works make up the repertoire.

Throughout the tours, workshops are a key feature of Transitions' stay in each venue, involving the dancers teaching and leading sessions based on the Company's performances, to students and other potential members of the audience.

The Company has a special commitment to excellence in the area of design and staging, and is a fine example of how a repertoire can adapt to a wide variety of spaces and situations. Their Production Manager, Lars Jensen, says, 'We plan our technical ideas in relation to the first-class facilities of the Bloomsbury Theatre. Obviously, these need to be scaled down for the studio theatres and school halls we may encounter on our tours. International touring has different requirements again'.

Transitions has the back-up of the Laban Centre's professional expertise, as well as its facilities. These factors are an essential feature of the group's success artistically and administratively, and its position within the organisation ensures its financial viability. The Head of Costume, who works with students, advises on designers for the group, and also organises the costume-making process.

As the company's activities fulfil the role of a fourth-year training course, the student dancers pay fees to the Centre. This factor, combined with the use of the on-site production facilities and studios, means that the group is largely self-financing. Revenue from performances is ploughed back into the Company, and the only real assistance, over and above this, comes from the British Council, who help support the overseas tours.

On tour in Britain, Transitions carries performers and a compact amount of its own equipment in a minibus and van, with Company Director, Production Manager and technician completing the group. It takes a grey portable floor and six LX stands, using 500 watt fresnels, which are usually placed three each side in the wings; visibility is the first priority in a venue with no equipment *in situ*, sidelighting only being effective against good general cover. The use of sculpting side light is not always appropriate to a work or venue; Lars Jensen comments, 'When sidelighting throws shadows on the walls, for example in old Corn Exchanges which are often very yellow inside, we only use overheads.' An 18-way, 2 pre-set manual dimmer board is carried to supplement existing equipment or used on its own if necessary. Sound is recorded on mini discs. None of the works has a set, a decision made for economic and practical reasons.

The company requires uninterrupted access to the performing area on the day of the show, heated changing and shower facilities adjacent to the performing area, full technical support from the venue and, when a 'fit-up' day is not included in the booking, the venue's technicians to pre-rig to the designer's lighting plan.

The company also carries four, multi purpose black 'legs', which may act as a screen for entrances and exits, mask an unneeded piano, or define the performing area in a school hall or gymnasium. In the case of setting up in a school, Lars, plus technician and school caretaker, will need access to the hall for the entire day. Once the stage is set up, the average 90 minute programme takes about three hours to run for spacing, and to allow the dancers to get used to the new performing area. This area needs to be a minimum of 8m × 7.5m (26.25 × 24.5ft).

Choreographers creating works for the 1996 programme were Aleta Hayes from the USA, Hervé Jourdet from France, Britain's David Massingham and Transitions' Company Director, American Bill Cratty. The programme contained a variety of styles and moods, music ranging from Mozart to The Carpenters, plus specially composed scores involving sampling and sound 'collage'. This diversity typified the range of musical sources and composition techniques currently used for dance and illustrates my point made in the first section, that choreographic style and intention will dictate many aspects of staging – including music and sound.

At Laban's Bonnie Bird Theatre and the Bloomsbury, the lighting rig allowed the three lighting designers to give each work a strongly individual look in terms of colour, mood and 'specials' used.

Aleta Hayes' work *Seele Brennt*, with costume designs by Suzie Holmes and lighting design by Anthony Bowne, had costumes for men and women in black and flesh colour. Suzie Holmes explored a subtle use of texture, using materials with contrasting matt and shiny qualities such as velvet, organza, satin and lycra, plus opaque and see-through looks, the use of pleating, and the occasional touch of sparkly fabric. This gave considerable variety within the total unified look. Costumes were clean in shape, the women in halter tops with an individual mini-skirt and bare legs. Men had sheer flesh-coloured tops and individual black trousers. Feet and footwear were featured, the dancers wearing varying styles but all with hard soles to enhance the sound of stamping feet. They appeared to combine the sound of Spanish or character shoes with the look of soft leather ankle boots. Towards the end a quiet moment occurred where the dancers took off their shoes, leaving them at the front of the stage in a ritualistic fashion, the remaining dance performed in bare feet. The lighting design gave a strongly edged, dramatic look, the textural quality of the costumes being echoed by lines of light on the floor from gobos. No colour was used, yet subtle shades of white, varying from candlelight yellow to almost ice-blue were achieved by the use of tungsten bulbs. Unlike halogen lamps, tungsten colour temperature depends on the wattage of the bulb and the level of intensity of the light. In *Seele Brennt* the back-lit cyc was never above 30%, at the 'yellower' end of the spectrum, whereas the lines on the floor were lit at 100%, creating sharp blue-white outlines.

Lars Jensen lit Hervé Jourdet's piece *Rève d'un petit chien*, taking the choreographer's influences as a starting point. These included Vaudeville, mythology, situations in Surrealist art and ideas of contorted bodies and 'freak' shows, the different elements existing in different time scales, reinforcing the overall atmosphere of absurdity and reminiscent of the dream of the title. The music created a forceful universe of sounds, using contemporary Spanish rock through general noise to Baroque. To create the Vaudeville atmosphere, Lars Jensen placed a number of tiny individual floor lights at the front of the stage as 'footlights'. An anarchic humour ran through the piece, the playfulness reflected in the *Brighton Rock* lighting of the floor – a pink base with white stripes.

The Peter Williams Design for Dance Project

Central Saint Martin's College of Art and Design, in London, features a specific project in dance design as part of its BA (Hons) degree in Theatre Design. The Design for Dance project offers opportunities for third-year design students to collaborate with student choreographers. The completed works are performed at the Cochrane Theatre in the Spring term. Choreography students come from several of the capital's leading vocational dance schools and colleges, each one creating its own short programme. Students are tutored by internationally reccognised designers in dance and theatre

The collaboration combines high artistic aims with the most stringent of budgets; many issues arise naturally as part of the process, which accurately reflects what happens 'in the real world'. Indeed, one of the main reasons for the project is to give prospective designers and choreographers a taste of reality, as well as to foster potential talent, and the issues which arise when two artistic disciplines meet are common ones in the staging process.

An initial meeting is arranged in the Autumn term of potential collaborators and their tutors. This ensures that designers and choreographers have sufficient time to get to know each other, explore creative possibilities and allow for the making up of the resulting set and costume designs. Costumes need to be worn and worked in, and the dancers need to try out elements of set design which may affect the amount or distribution of dancing space. In particular, sets involving constructions on, in or through which the dancers move, need plenty of time to be tried out. Safety, as well as aesthetic considerations are paramount, and constructions, as well as costumes, may need to be adjusted to suit the dancers.

The aim of genuine collaboration is that each art makes an equal contribution, but it is likely that one or the other will have the initial idea, which will be taken up by both parties and freely explored.

In the 1996 project, one piece included a Japanese ghost story, telling of a child with no face, the *Nopperabo* of the title, who is rejected by her peers. This provided interesting design challenges and time was spent exploring the Japanese influence, as well as the notion of rejection and, of course, the 'no face'. Choreographer Rieko Nagabuchi chose music by Bela Bartok, and designer Bridget Chew decided to opt for a universal treatment of the theme in her designs. She took shapes from Japanese headwear to create striking wigs for the dancers, and mirrored these in the introduction of lightweight 'boxes' which were suspended in a line at head height, from a bar. These divided the stage space from front to back and suggested children's hanging mobiles or kites, with the straight line almost constituting a set of 'railings'. The dancers ran in and out of these boxes/railings, tapping them playfully, making them spin, those with faces putting their heads inside the boxes, thereby becoming 'no faces', too! On the practical side, it took a number of attempts to come up with an effective and suitable treatment of the 'no face' for the dancer in the title role. The combination of needing to eliminate the features, yet not to create a skull-like look, and the necessity of allowing the dancer to see, proved a challenging task. Even at the dress rehearsal, adjustments were being made, after the discovery that the strong stage lighting virtually blinded the dancer with 'no face'. Her role included slow adagio sections, where balance and control had to be maintained, no easy feat when wearing a mask and in bright light!

Another piece *Bodily Harm*, was a solo choreographed and danced by Richard O'Brien, who also wrote the poetic text spoken onstage by an actress. This resulted in a physical and vocal dialogue between the two, and the piece included images of 'falling'. Physical, emotional and mental aspects of falling were explored in dance and speech, and such was the inevitable importance of the floor, ground or landing point that designer Anna Fleischle chose to cover part of the dancing space with red earth – actual soil which was sprinkled onto the stage. Richard's costume was a basic pair of trunks with a thick application of body paint in an unearthly pale shade of flesh. Movements into and including the soil, and the use of bare flesh, heightened the contrast between the airy height of the point from which the falling commenced and the tactile, earthy ground on which it finished. The conflict between flesh and spirit was poetically evoked.

Nopperabo: *Central St Martin's Design for Dance Project 1996,* described on page 120
(PHOTO: *Tim Griffiths*)

Practically, the work had to be placed last, because of the time it took to sweep the floor completely clear of soil! The floor also needed a wash and sufficient time to dry.

Staging a traditional ballet on student dancers

Anyone staging one of the well-known nineteenth-century ballets will need to have had considerable experience with a major company and may be invited to mount all, or part, of a classic for the annual performance of a vocational dance school, with a cast of graduate students.

Young dancers need the challenge of a classic – it provides a yardstick by which to assess potential and achievement. However, it can be so testing that mounting even a short extract should be carefully considered. Will the dancers be able to get through the work, let alone do it justice? Decisions concerning artistic integrity must be made, and a fine line drawn between providing a needed opportunity, and finding trainees who are really ready. Will the presentation honour the choreographer's vision and enhance public perception of the work?

Only a handful of students, annually, will make a living in ballet, most graduates moving into modern dance, musical theatre or other stage branches; but vocational schools offer ballet as an important part of broader training alongside other dance techniques, drama and singing. It is, therefore, prudent to assess whether the current graduates will be able to stand up to the rigours of performing a classic, or whether they would be better served by having a ballet created especially for them. A work by a good choreographer will show off the dancers' abilities whilst challenging them, and the audience may prefer to see the dancers shine, rather than be on tenterhooks watching a classic, wondering if the dancers will 'make it' to the end.

A traditional version or your own? A distinction should be made between presenting the traditional choreography – 'after Petipa' – of, say, *The Nutcracker* – and choreographing one's own version, using Tchaikovsky's music. The latter seems daunting, but might be more successful in the long run. By not competing with an established version, a choreographer can capitalise on the dancers' abilities. Petipa's version could, however, be taken as a model, the scenario and traditional dances offering plenty of scope for individual interpretation. The Mirlitons, for instance, could be danced by young teenagers, using very simple *pointe* work. The *demi-caractère* Chinese dance lends itself to children, teenagers or adults; strapping lads could make a show-stopper of the Russian dance, and the first act contains specific roles for children – Clara, Fritz and their friends. The Snowflakes could be eager eight-year-olds, who might even contribute a few choreographic ideas of their own; or it might be the very thing for older students to learn how to work as a professionally disciplined *corps de ballet*. King Rat offers a splendid chance for an energetic, dramatic character dance of either sex – and so on. The point is that, if you cannot comfortably cast an 'authentic' version of a classic, it might be better to create your own.

A good producer If a vocational school is to stage a classical extract, then the value of a good producer cannot be overestimated. It is invaluable for students to be coached by a professional dancer. Most dancers have great respect for the work they are passing on, and treat their protegés with loving concern, being acutely aware of how it feels to be on the receiving end of advice and criticism.

   However, if they come directly from a performing career, with little experience of teaching, they may be at a loss when faced with students who do not match up to the company dancers to whom they are accustomed. Some ex-professionals are natural teachers and coaches, whilst others have neither the flair, nor the endless patience needed, to get the best out of their charges. Although students must be stretched and challenged, the demands must not exceed what can realistically be expected.

Casting Once a trustworthy producer is found, the first task will be to cast principal and solo roles, and the *corps de ballet*. Auditioning and 'trying out' can be stressful for young dancers, so watching a daily technique or repertoire class, might work well with the youngest ones. For older students a 'mini-audition' could be set up. An audition conducted in a relaxed, yet efficient atmosphere will allow the auditionees to show their best work; a certain amount of adrenaline and excitement is positive, helping students discover abilities in themselves they might not have suspected. However, a row of stony faces watching, who appear to seek faults rather than an enjoyable performance, can make even an assured young dancer falter. Hardened professionals, let along young students, need a huge amount of physical, emotional and mental energy to tackle the classics, and they must be given the confidence and will to succeed.

Principal roles When casting principal roles, qualities to look for are an adequate technique (which will not fail under pressure, excitement or fatigue), musicality and expressiveness, and a physique neither injury-prone nor lacking in stamina. The dancers should also genuinely enjoy performing, and be at home onstage, this factor being difficult to assess outside an actual performance situation. It is surprising what happens to a dancer onstage, with the most extrovert student in the class-room failing to 'come across', or an indifferent character suddenly catching everyone's eye. Whether this is due to charisma or stage presence, it is a real asset. Some dancers have great conviction in their work and a deep desire to communicate with an audience; adrenaline can give an intensity and edge to one performer, whilst another appears to withdraw 'behind a veil'; some try too hard, forcing their performance and others lose their nerve. There are natural performers and those who fall apart onstage and it is important to bear this in mind when casting. Ballet can get bogged down in the class-room with the acquisition of technical skills but these are only a means to an end, and the end takes place onstage!

Student dancers must also be able to absorb and reflect stylistic subtleties in the choreography – not always easy – the Romantic style of *Giselle* or *La Sylphide*, for example, being notoriously difficult. A further consideration is that of partnership, as the classics generally have a ballerina and *danseur noble* in the leading roles, and the two must look and work well together, physically and temperamentally.

The Arts Educational London Schools staging of The Kingdom of the Shades from La Bayadère

The Arts Educational Schools in London offer full-time courses in dance, drama and musical theatre. The Senior School's Dancers' Course traditionally includes a classical extract in its annual performance, alongside a strong modern dance element. The Kingdom of the Shades section from Petipa's *La Bayadère* (1877) was chosen for the 1996 programme, arranged and staged by tutors Judith Maden and Michael Woodward. Judith Maden, former principal dancer with the Royal Ballet, teaches repertoire to the Arts Educational students. 'This year, the choice of *Bayadère* came out of the repertoire classes, as the solos were featured as part of the 2nd year students' ballet assessments. The entry of the *corps de ballet* of Shades is one of the most famous moments in Petipa's work and a great challenge to young dancers, so the scene seemed to be ideal for performance.'

The entry involves the entire female *corps* taking slow *arabesques en fondu* down a ramp at the back of the stage and continuing in a serpentine floor pattern until all the dancers are on, filling the stage with the purest classical lines. Set at night, the dancers dressed in short white tutus, it is the epitome of Petipa's classicism. From the dancers' point of view, it is a keen challenge – the leading *corps de ballet* dancer does thirty-two *arabesques* during the entry alone! Lines are formal and the *corps* must work 'as one body', feeling and breathing with the music together. The years of class-room discipline come to fruition in this extract, and one dancer off the music or 'out of sync.' can destroy the whole spellbinding effect. Whilst the demands are intense, the magic of working as a group to create the rarefied atmosphere, with its precision and absorption, is a powerful reward. Judith Maden comments: 'Whether or not the students are going to become ballet dancers, the only way they will really understand what their class-room training is for, is to experience both the difficulties and the magic of dancing in such a piece.'

Great stamina and physical strength are needed to sustain the classical line and maintain the ethereal look, and the three solos are ruthlessly revealing – even the tiniest linking step must be as pure and faultless as the highlights.

The Arts Educational students have their own theatre on site. The dancers have plenty of opportunity to rehearse onstage, and to observe their classmates 'from out front', seeing the effect from the audience's point of view.

Di Steadman and Claire Wilson, are involved in the design of lighting and costumes, respectively. Claire Wilson said

> Each show must be of a high standard, as it is a showcase for the students and their first exposure to agents. We have a vast stock of costumes, and the tutors have contacts with dance companies from whom we occasionally borrow. However, we invest in each production, making something new, and re-using items in stock. In the case of *Bayadère*, we had tutus from a previous staging of *Swan Lake*, which had been designed to be longer than usual – the 'Degas' length. Twelve of these could be reused, shortening the skirts and refitting bodices. We them made one set of new bodices and two sets of skirts. It is vital to make a tutu correctly – it is such a precise art that the experts will know if it is wrong.

Di Steadman designed the dance lighting rig when the former gymnasium was converted into the studio theatre. She lights each new work in collaboration with the choreographer, also taking on a tutorial role with students who may have a dance being performed. In this case she prefers to see the piece first, then talk to the student, observing that novices frequently want too many cues for the length of a dance. A new show takes two days to light, each work allotted two hours, and she requests that choreographers notify here of any 'specials' needed two weeks in advance.

Royal Ballet Education Projects

*Samsara **The Cycle of Life*** Darryl Jaffray, Head of Education (Ballet) at The Royal Opera House says,

> The education work of the professional dance companies is continually developing, as education officers find new ways of exploring the possibilities of their company's particular genre. Sacred Waters, Sacred Lands was an innovative project inspired by the 'Sacred Lands Devoted Lives' exhibition at the Horniman Museum, bringing together The Royal Ballet, Academy of Indian Dance, and the Horniman Museum and directed by representatives from these three organisations*

Supported by The Esmée Fairbairn Charitable Trust, The Friends of Covent Garden and Lewisham Theatre, the project involved students from five secondary schools in south-east London in the creation of a dance for performance at Lewisham Theatre.

Samsara involved the teenagers in the creation of dance, music and design assisted by specialists from the Royal Ballet and their own teachers. Spanning eighteen months from planning stage to final performance, the actual creative period was just eight weeks, with each art form allotted an hour and a half a week.

The teachers' pack described the project as follows:

> Working across the curriculum to involve the expressive arts and humanities courses, students will explore ways in which the elements of fire, water, earth and air have been expressed in religious ritual and art from South Asia and Europe, to work towards a performance and exhibition event. In particular, the dance aspect

*'Sacred Waters, Sacred Lands', *The Dancing Times*, July 1995

will draw on the basic elements of shape, rhythm and gesture of both classical ballet and Indian dance to create a dance production with costume, set design and music.

Several schools were working on GCSE Dance, one group using the experience as part of their coursework.

It was proposed that the specialist workshop leaders guide and stimulate, but leave the actual work to evolve from the students' own ideas.

In movement terms, the two dance disciplines of ballet and Bharata Natyam were incorporated in simple forms into warm-up sequences and used as material from which the students could draw inspiration – for instance, a step pattern from the South Asian style might be used as a starting point for improvisation. Rachel Lightfoot explained:

> We explored different aspects of the *Samsara* cycle, starting with largely literal, mime-based ideas, out of which we spent time abstracting movement possibilities. We also used speech and conversation as a starting point, adding gesture, and then taking away the voice and just using movements developed from the gestures to express the conversation. In the Dawn and Childhood section, we included children's games as one source of inspiration, and in all sections we used imagery to fire the students' imaginations.

Samsara music was guided by Jonathan Petter and Ansuman Biswas, each school using the weekly ninety minutes differently, one group having both dance and music within the same lesson, with each art form having only half as much time and input as the other schools. However, Jonathan Petter found that, paradoxically, this worked well, resulting in moments like the wedding procession where the students moved and played simultaneously. Another school had dance and music on consecutive days, allowing him to pass on what had been achieved from one lesson to the next. In the early stages, he says:

> Much time was spent allowing the students to experience what it means to take part in a group performance, getting the feeling of really working together, and enjoying the buzz when it works. They spent as much time as possible actually playing and having to maintain concentration for substantial periods. Each instrumental sound was important in its own right, so every student had a responsibility to the whole. Getting the 'Wow!' going – that fantastic feeling when the whole group has pulled together and made it work – was very important. We started out with simple rhythmic patterns before moving on to the complexities of Indian music. In India, dancers and musicians both learn to speak rhythms, so we used this idea in *Samsara*. We would take a bols, a spoken Indian rhythm, and develop it in movement terms. Each sound has a corresponding percussion stroke, each syllable representing a different sound on the drum, and so the musicians would take a bols and use it to generate a tune or rhythm. We also used the doubling-up common in Indian music, where a rhythm pattern repeats at double speed before returning to the original. In order to allow for the length of the music to fit with the dance, we tended to work in repeated patterns, so that we could add or subtract when the time came.
>
> With the four seasons and elements in the cycle, it was important to make each section distinctive musically, so we developed an individual sound palette for each one as well as using a different rhythm pattern, one group using an Indian

scale and four time, another using a three, or a seven and so on. Instrumentally we had the resources of the schools supplemented by the Academy of Indian Dance, and sounds included skin sounds from the various drums; metallic hand cymbals, chimes, gongs and bowls, electric keyboards, and basic shakers, woodblocks and maracas. As well as conducting, Ansuman and I also played along, adding clarinet and saxophone.

Designs for the project were initiated and guided by artist Bhajan Hunjan and theatre designer Francis O'Connor. The Horniman exhibition featured life in a South Asian village and this inspired one of the most striking aspects of the *Samsara* stage set. Hindu worship involved women making a design on the floor of their home using rice flour and water. Traditionally a circular pattern is used and this was taken by Bhajan Hunjan as a starting point for the creation of a stage floor painting. Planned and executed by the students under her guidance, water-based paints were applied directly to a circular piece of dance linoleum, which was eventually glued down onto the larger dance floor in the theatre, creating a vivid and colourful focal point of the set design – see front cover illustration.

Other elements of the set inspired by the cyclic idea included a circular screen which could be hung vertically, horizontally, at an angle or flown out entirely. When vertically hung, it was used for the projection of hand-painted glass slides, and when horizontal became a table. Each school made one major part of the set – whether producing the slides, the floor painting or the canopy for the wedding scene. They also made one of four perspex boxes representing a season, which were placed in a square on the stage, each containing a long narrow perspex screen which unravelled as the relevant school and season appeared. Each school designed one main costume, with all making the hand-held papier-mâché masks, and two ore three face masks, the chief one of which was worn by the Fire character and made by Bhajan. Costume basics included all-in-ones, waistcoats, T-shirts and baggy shalwar-style trousers.

Bhajan and Francis needed to consider all aspects of set and costumes for effectiveness and practicality when they were to be created within a strict school timetable. Resources at Lewisham Theatre had to be taken into consideration. It was decided to build a special thrust stage to include an entrance through the auditorium as well as at the sides, creating a walkway along which musicians and dancers could move in a procession. Foot-high platforms on either side of the stage seated the different groups of musicians, enabling them to see the action, yet not block the audience's view. Staging features included musical instruments being carried onstage in a basket as part of the wedding scene and being given out to the players as the long colourful silk scarves were hung up in celebration .

Joyce Butler School of Dancing

There are remarkable individuals who do everything described in this book and do it with children, some as young as four years old! One such person is Joyce Butler, who has taught children to dance for the past sixty years. Her school caters for boys and girls from 3 years upwards, and they learn ballet, tap, modern, Greek and national dance. Learning to dance for the sheer joy and fun of it is open to every child.

Part of the year's curriculum includes a performance in the local theatre and the timetable is arranged so that examination work is completed by the time rehearsals are seriously under way. Every child takes part in the show, which means that each year's cast comprises around 200. Performances on this scale need to be organised like a military operation.

Children nowadays enjoy a wide variety of pastimes, from swimming to piano lessons, and dancing classes have to be fitted into their busy schedule. Joyce Butler's pupils dance for one hour a week, and it is within this time scale that exam and performance work must be completed. This would be impossible without commitment and discipline from the children, and Miss Butler establishes these qualities from the beginning. Anyone who has worked with young children understands the delicate balance needed to maintain youthful high spirits and the joy of dancing, whilst installing a respect and discipline towards the art form, as well as towards teachers and fellow pupils. She achieves this through fostering a relaxed but close involvement from the parents. At the end of the year, each pupil votes for the recipients of the school's Fellowship Cups, awarded to those who, in the opinion of the children, have been the most helpful and co-operative. The best dancers do not always win the prizes, and this establishes a value for consideration and teamwork – crucial qualities for anyone hoping to work in the theatre.

With this background, the foundation is laid for the achievement of the seemingly impossible – an evening's performance, fully choreographed and costumed, and involving all the children. Rehearsals begin in the February prior to the May or June show; a quartet of teachers and Miss Butler herself devise individual dances, and at this early stage, with the exam preparation still taking priority, the rehearsals for trying out ideas and deciding what will suit each group. Whilst the level of each class dictates what can be achieved, dances still need to be skillfully put together, particularly with the youngest children. They may be 4 or 5 years old, and the sheer novelty of being on a stage, in theatre lighting and with a big black void out front, can make even the most confident child lose concentration. Therefore dances are arranged so that the children are able to get on and off stage easily, can watch each other during the piece, relate securely to the music and have a jolly good time!

Music is largely live, with pianist Mrs Newlyn arranging and adapting classical piano pieces. Like all good dance musicians, she lovingly watches the children as she plays, following and supporting them throughout each rehearsal. Modern and tap numbers are generally on tape.

The fun of dressing up in costume is one of the most exciting parts. Joyce Butler tackles the task of finding upwards of a hundred costumes with her customary flair for involving people and channelling expertise. She simply ask the Mums to make their child's costumes! If it involves making, say, a dress, then one mum will make up an example, which will be passed around as a pattern. Several skilled dressmakers amongst the mothers can advise if necessary. As the performance date nears, everyone pulls together and, at the last studio rehearsal, elaborate costumes miraculously start to appear. A Ukrainian national dance is to be performed for the first time, and the richly decorated bodices, skirts and aprons, and beribboned headdresses are proudly shown off. Teachers working with the youngest children take them through their dances several times, each with a different 'front', so they will not be disoriented when faced with the stage. After the finale, the huge cast packs into the hall. After a run-through and notes, parents are also invited in, and everyone sits down to listen to information about the Monday evening Dress Rehearsal in the theatre. Times of arrival are given out and where to change, mums being allowed backstage for the dress rehearsal but not for the actual performances.

Trying out headdresses, Joyce Butler School of Dancing (PHOTO: *Mike Concah*)

All costumes, especially tutus, must be marked with the owner's name, and each dance is talked through to clarify requirements for socks, shoes, tights and hairdos. Older girls are swift to point out quick changes and those needing a different hairstyle. It is at this point, when the entire company is assembled together, that skills in polite mob control are needed and Joyce Butler's co-teachers start to take on the roles of chaperones, stage managers, hairdressers, make-up artists and first-aiders. They are also required to explain how to get to the theatre by car, train, bus or cab, where to park and how to find the stage door. These and other roles will continue until after the last performance.

Once in the theatre, each dressing room has four helpers/dressers, with more for the baby class. The babies are in a room of their own, with colouring books, pencils and other amusements available to keep them occupied until it is their turn. Their dances are always in the first half, so that they can be taken home at a reasonable hour. It is suggested that the children arrive at the theatre with their hair and make-up already done, but if this is impossible, one of the helpers will take over.

Staging dance with children is no different from working with adults from the production point of view – the same standards of sound quality, stage management and other aspects apply, possibly even better ones, as a young child may not be able to 'busk it', as an adult would, if something goes wrong. Children cannot be expected to work long and late hours; large casts will need long breaks if they have to queue for food and drink. There need to be sufficient toilets handy. How the children are to find their way round backstage areas needs consideration, and dropping-off and picking-up points and times need to be defined. Apart from that, it is only the larger number of helpers which may make a school performance obviously different from an 'adult' production.

APPENDIX

Film/video resources
Apply for details to

Dance Books Ltd
15 Cecil Court
London WC2N 4EZ tel: 0171-836 2314 fax: 0171-212 9410

National Resource Centre for Dance
University of Surrey
Guildford, Surrey GU2 5XH tel: (01483) 259316 fax: (01483) 259500

The Dancing Times Ltd
45-47 Clerkenwell Green
London EC1R 0EB tel: 0171-250 3006 fax: 0171-253 6679

The Dream (Frederick Ashton) is available as part of a teacher's resource pack on
The Dream from
Education Department
Royal Opera House
Covent Garden
London WC2E 9DD

Dance programmes on film (cinema and TV) and video may be viewed by serious researchers at the National Film Archive, part of the British Film Institute, 21 Stephen Street, London W1P 1PL (tel: 0171-255 1444, ext. 323; fax: 0171-580 7503). Viewing must take place on the premises and is strictly by appointment. A charge is made for the service. The charge is waived for members of The Society for Dance Research on production of their current membership card. The Society for Dance Research, 9 Cecil Court, London WC2N 4EZ.

Bibliography and further reading

GENERAL
Banes, Sally, *Terpsichore in Sneakers* (1980), Boston: Houghton Mifflin
Bland, Alexander, *The Royal Ballet: The First Fifty Years* (1981)
Brown, Jean Morrison, *The Vision of Modern Dance* (1980), London: Dance Books
Clarke, Mary, and Clement Crisp, *Ballet: an illustrated history* (1962), London: A & C Black
Clarke, Mary, and Clement Crisp, *London Contemporary Dance Theatre: the first 21 years* (1989), London: Dance Books
Cohen, Selma Jeanne, ed., *The Modern Dance: seven statements of belief* (1965), Connecticut: Wesleyan University Press
Cohen, Selma Jeanne, ed., *Dance as a Theatre Art* (1974), New York: Dodd, Mead & Co.
Cunningham, Merce, and Jacqueline Lesschaeve, *The Dancer and the Dance* (1985), London: Marion Boyars
Davies, Mollie, *Helping Children to Learn through a Movement Perspective* (1995), London: Hodder & Stoughton
Denby, Edwin, *Dancers, Buildings and People in the Street* ((1965), New York: Horizon Press
Ellfeldt, Lois, *Dance from Magic to Art* (1976), Iowa: Wm C. Brown
Goodwin, Noel, *A Ballet for Scotland* (1979), Edinburgh: Canongate Press
Graham, Martha, *Blood Memory* (1992), London: Macmillan
Guest, Ivor, *The Dancer's Heritage: a short history of ballet* (1988), The Dancing Times

Jordan, Stephanie, *Striding Out* (1992), London: Dance Books
Jowitt, Deborah, *Time and the Dancing Image* (1988), New York: Wm Morrow
Kirstein, Lincoln, *Movement and Metaphor* (1971), London: Pitman Publishing
Mackrell, Judith, *Out of Line* (1992), London: Dance Books
Mille, Agnes de, *To a Young Dancer* (1962), USA Atlantic: Little, Brown
Pritchard, Jane, *Rambert: a celebration* (1996), London: Rambert Dance Company
Preston-Dunlop, Valerie, *Dance Words* (1995), Harwood: Academic Publishers
Rambert, Marie, *Quicksilver* (1972), London: Macmillan
Stearn, Marshall and Jean, *Jazz Dance: the story of vernacular dance* (1968), London: Macmillan
Stodelle, Ernestine, *Deep Song: the dance story of Martha Graham* (1984), London: Collier Macmillan
Taper, Bernard, *Balanchine* (1974), New York: Macmillan
Valois, Ninette de, *Invitation to the Ballet* (1937), London: The Bodley Head
Valois, Ninette de, *Come Dance with Me* (1957), London: Hamish Hamilton
Valois, Ninette de, *Step by Step* (1977), London: W. H. Allen
White, Joan W., ed., *Twentieth-century Dance in Britain* (1985), London: Dance Books

CHOREOGRAPHY
Chaplin, L., and L. T. Blom, *The Intimate Act of Choreography* (1989), London: Dance Books
Cunningham, Merce, ed., and Frances Starr, *Changes: notes on choreography* (1968), New York: Something Else Press
Graham, Martha, *The Notebooks of Martha Graham* (1973), New York: Harcourt Brace Jovanovich
Hayes, Elizabeth R., *Dance Composition and Production* (1993), New Jersey: Princeton Book Co.
Humphrey, Doris, *The Art of Making Dances* (1959), London: Dance Books
Smith-Autard, Jacqueline M., *Dance Composition* (1996), London: A & C Black
Turner, Margery, with Ruth Grauert, *New Dance: approaches to nonliteral choreography* (1971), University of Pittsburgh Press
Whitley, Ann, *Look before you Leap: an advice and rights guide for choreographers* (1995), London: Dance UK

MUSIC
Cage, John, *Silence: lectures and writings* (1987), London: Marion Boyars
Copland, Aaron, *Music and Imagination* (1952), Harvard University Press
Evans, Edwin, *Music and the Dance*, London: Herbert Jenkins
Sawyer, Elizabeth, *Dance with the Music: the world of the ballet musician* (1985), Cambridge University Press
Teck, Katherine, *Music for the Dance* (1989), Connecticut: Greenwood Press
Teck, Katherine, *Movement to Music* (1990), Connecticut: Greenwood Press
Teck, Katherine, *Ear Training for the Body* (1994), New Jersey: Princeton Book Co.
Walne, Graham, *Sound for the Theatre* (1990), London: A & C Black

DESIGN AND COSTUMES
Baygan, Lee, *Make-up for Theatre, Film and Televison*, London: A & C Black
Bentley, Toni, *Costumes by Karinska* (1995), New York: Harry N. Abrams
Clarke, Mary, and Clement Crisp, *Design for Ballet* (1978), London: Studio Vista
Docherty, Peter, and Tim White, eds, *From Diaghilev to the Pet Shop Boys* (1996), London: Lund Humphries
Martin, Rupert, ed., *Artists Design for Dance 1909–1984* (1984), Bristol: Arnolfini Gallery
Reid, Francis, *Designing for the Theatre* (1996), London: A & C Black
Rowell, Kenneth, *Stage Design* (1968), London: Studio Vista
Strong, Roy, with Richard Buckle and Ivor Guest, *Designing for the Dancer* (1981), London: Elron Press
Swinfield, Rosemarie, *Stage Make-up Step-by-Step* (1995), London: A & C Black
Thomas, Terry, *Create Your Own Stage Sets* (1985), London: A & C Black

Williams, Peter, *Masterpieces of Ballet Design* (1992), Oxford: Phaidon Press

LIGHTING
Reid, Francis, *Discovering Stage Lighting* (1993), London: Focal Press
Reid, Francis, *Lighting the Stage* (1995), London: Focal Press
Reid, Francis, *The Stage Lighting Handbook* (1996), London: A & C Black
Rosenthal, Jean, and Lael Wertenbaker, *The Magic of Light* (1973), Mass.: Little, Brown & Co.

STAGE MANAGEMENT AND PRODUCTION
Bond, Daniel, *Stage Management: a gentle art* (1997), London: A & C Black
Ramsden, Timothy, and Pauline Courtice, *Stagecraft*
Reid, Francis, *The Staging Handbook* (1995), London: A & C Black
Walne, Graham, ed., *Effects for the Theatre* (1995), London: A & C Black

FUNDING
The Arts Funding Guide, Directory of Social Change (Publications Department), 24 Stephenson Way, London NW1 2DP
Courrier d'Europe, 126 rue Franklin, Brussels 1040, Belgium
European Guide to Foundations and Sponsors, International Arts Bureau, tel: 0171-403 7001
The Hollis Arts Funding Handbook, Hollis Directories Ltd, Harlequin House, 7 High Street, Teddington, Middlesex TW11 8EL (published annually)

PUBLICITY
Sharman, Helen, *Bums on Seats: how to publicise your show* (1992), London: A & C Black

ARCHITECTURE AND FLOORING
Armstrong, Leslie, and Roger Morgan, *Space for Dance* (1984), US Publishing Center for Cultural Resources
Foley, Mark, *Dance Spaces* (1994), London: The Arts Council of England
Foley, Mark, *A Handbook for Dance Floors* (1995), London: Dance UK

HEALTH FOR DANCERS
Brinson, Peter, and Fiona Dick, Fit to Dance? (1996), London: Gulbenkian Foundation
Fay, Maria, *Mind over Body* (1997), London: A & C Black
Gelb, Michael, *Body Learning* (1981), London: Aurum Press
Howse, Justin, and Shirley Hancock, *Dance Technique and Injury Prevention* (1992), London: A & C Black
Ponder, Catherine, *The Healing Secret of the Ages* (1981), A. Thomas & Co.
Ryan, Allan J., and Robert E. Stephens, eds, *The Healthy Dancer* (1989), London: Dance Books

Useful addresses

ABSA (Association of Business Sponsorship of the Arts)
Nutmeg House
60 Gainsford Street
Butlers Wharf
London SE1 2NY

Academy of Indian Dance
16 Flaxman Terrace
London WC1H 9AT

Arts Council of England
14 Great Peter Street
London SW1P 3NQ

Arts Council of Northern Ireland
181a Stranmills Road
Belfast BT9 5DU

The Arts Educational London Schools
Cone Ripman House
14 Bath Road
London W4 1LY

British Performing Arts Medicine Trust
18 Ogle Street
London W1P 7LG

Borovick Fabrics Ltd
Berwick Street
London W1

Central St Martin's College of Art and Design
Southampton Row
London WC1

Dance Books Ltd
15 Cecil Court
London WC2N 4EZ

Dance Council of Ireland
65 Fitzwilliam Square
Dublin 2

Dance UK
23 Crisp Road
London W6 9RL

Dance Umbrella
20 Chancellor's Street
London W6 9RN

The DancXchange
Birmingham Hippodrome
Hurst Street
Birmingham B5 4TB

DV8 Physical Theatre
Artsadmin Toynbee Studios
28 Commercial Street
London E1 6LS

The Educational Recording Agency
33-34 Alfred Place
London WC1E 7DP

English National Ballet
Markova House
39 Jay Mews
London SW7 2ES

Focus on Dance
Bullimores House
Church Lane
Cranleigh
Surrey GU6 8AS

Foundation for Community Dance
13–15 Belvoir Street
Leicester
LE7 9SU

Greasepaint School of Stage, TV and Film
   Make-Up
143 Northfield Avenue
London W13

Green Candle Dance Company
309 Aberdeen House
22 Highbury Grove
London N5 2EA

Independent Theatre Council
12 The Leathermarket
Weston Street
London SE1 3ER

International Arts Bureau
4 Baden Place
Crosby Row
London SE1 1YW

The Jiving Lindy Hoppers
35 Newton Avenue
Acton
London W3 8AR

Joyce Butler School of Dancing
St Paul's Hall
West Ealing
London W13

Mechanical Copyright Protection Society
Elgar House
41 Streatham High Street
London SW16 1ER

MacCulloch and Wallis Ltd
25 Dering Street
London W1

Harold Moore Records
Great Marlborough Street
London W1

National Resource Centre for Dance
University of Surrey
Guildford
Surrey GU2 5XH

The Performing Right Society
29-33 Berners Street
London W1P 4AA

Phonographic Performance Ltd
Ganton House
14–22 Ganton Street
London W1V 1LB

The Place Dance Services
The Place
17 Duke's Road
London WC1H 9AB

RDC Physiotherapy Clinic
32 Wimpole Street
London W1M 7AE

Royal Academy of Dancing
36 Battersea Square
London SW11 3RA

The Royal Ballet Education Department
Royal Opera House
Covent Garden
London WC2E 7QA

Scottish Arts Council
12 Manor Place
Edinburgh EH3 7DD

Transitions Dance Company
Laban Centre for Movement and Dance
Laurie Grove
London SE14

Whaley's (Bradford) Ltd
Harris Court
Great Horton
Bradford
West Yorkshire

Welsh Arts Council
Holst House
Museum Place
Cardiff CF1 3NX

NATIONAL DANCE AGENCIES
Dance 4
3–9 Hockley
Nottingham NG1 1FH

Dance City
Peel Lane
off Waterloo Street
Newcastle upon Tyne NE1 4DW

The DanceXchange – see above

North West National Dance Agency
PO Box 19
Winsford
Cheshire CW7 2AS

The Place – see above

Suffolk Dance
The Performing Arts Centre
Sidegate Lane
Ipswich IP4 3DL

Thamesdown National Dance Agency
Town Hall Studios
Regent Circus
Swindon
Wilts

Yorkshire Dance Centre
3 St Peters Buildings
St Peters Square
Leeds LS9 8AH

Addresses in the USA

See listings provided by
Stern's Performing Arts Directory
33 West 60 Street
New York, NY 10023

and also
ASCAP
1 Lincoln Plaza
New York City

Joseph Patelson Music House
160 West 56 Street
New York,

Princeton Book Company
P.O. Box 57
Pennington, NJ 08534

Regional Dance of America
c/o Allegro Academy of Dance
1570 S., Dairy Ashford – Suite 200
Houston, TX 77077

INDEX